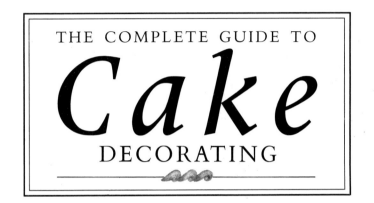

THE COMPLETE GUIDE TO

Cake

DECORATING

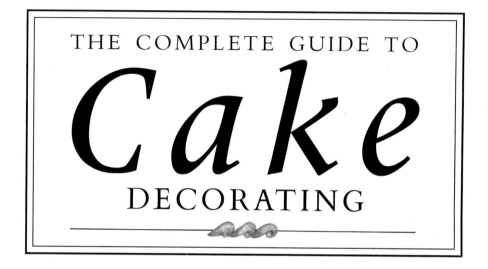

THE COMPLETE GUIDE TO
Cake
DECORATING

Introduction by Janice Murfitt · Edited by Deborah Gray

MEREHURST

LONDON

This edition published 1990 by
Merehurst Limited, Ferry House, 51-57 Lacy Road,
Putney, London SW15 1PR

© Copyright 1990 Merehurst Limited

Reprinted 1991

ISBN 1-85391-139-9

Edited by Deborah Gray
Designed by Clive Dorman
Jacket design by Bridgewater Design
Special photography by Helen Pask
Jacket photography by Guy Rycart
Typeset by Avocet Robinson, Buckingham
Colour separation by Fotographics Ltd., London – Hong Kong
Printed in Italy by New Interlitho S.p.A., Milan

The Publishers would like to thank the following for their help
and contributions to the book:

Cake Flair, 230 Upper Richmond Road, Putney, London SW15
David Mellor, 4 Sloane Square, London SW1W 8EE and 66 King Street,
Manchester M2 4NP

CONTENTS

INTRODUCTION

Cake decorating is an art to be enjoyed in our own homes when the time is available and the occasion arises. It is often regarded as a hobby by those who enjoy it, but a daunting prospect for many people not experienced in this art. It is a complex subject and needs to be mastered in stages, but when approached with confidence and patience, it is possible to achieve a very satisfying and rewarding result with the use of a few simple materials and some basic equipment.

This book has been designed to show you, step-by-step, how to progress from making, icing and decorating the simplest sponge cake to a very elaborate wedding cake. The most important step is to make a cake worthy to be iced and decorated. Recipes are given for many shapes and sizes of cakes from a plain sponge to a rich, traditional fruit cake.

Simple icings and frosting are included for basic cake decorating, and explicit instructions given on how to marzipan, royal ice and sugarpaste cakes giving a perfect surface on which to apply the finished design.

Decorating and finishing touches have been approached with great thought, giving simple finishes with the use of silk or fresh flowers, ribbons, bows and ready-made decorations. Other sections include sugarpaste designs using cutout pieces, moulded decorations, frills and flowers, followed by sections on piping and more advanced icing work.

With patience, practice and the aid of this book, you will be able to produce cakes which are admired by all at special occasions.

JANICE MURFITT

GETTING STARTED

Like all hobbies, cake decorating does require some special equipment. However, initially you will need very little to get started, and then as you become more adventurous, you will gradually build up your collection of piping tubes, colours, cutters and other specialist equipment.

Cake design is also covered in this chapter. A good cake is always planned in advance, so that the colours, density of design and the decorations all complement each other. If the cake is to be the focal point then it is also important to ensure that the cake stand and accessories match the mood of the cake. All these factors are dealt with in this chapter.

EQUIPMENT

Most tools used for sugarcraft are ordinary kitchen equipment. The more specialist tools can be found in a good cake decorating shop.

Ball tools: A selection of different sizes are required although a glass-headed pin stuck into a piece of dowelling can be used in place of a small ball tool.

Bowls: A selection of various sizes, preferably glass, all clean and free of grease.

Brushes: Use sable-hair brushes for the best effect and have several different sizes to hand.

Cake boards: These come in a wide variety of shapes and sizes designed to correspond with the various cake tins (pans) on the market.

Cocktail sticks (toothpicks): Used to add colouring paste to icing and in modelling work. Japanese birch are the best quality sticks that are available.

Crimpers and leather embossing tools: Used for decorating sugarpaste and marzipan.

Cutters: A wide selection of cutters is useful. Flower, pastry, sweet (candy) and biscuit (cookie) cutters are used for making plaques and cutouts, while frills and flounces are made with Garrett cutters.

Electric mixer: Useful in cake preparation and for making royal icing.

Florist's wire: You will need varying gauges for flower work, and modelling.

Knives: A good kitchen knife with a fine sharp blade is essential, you may also wish to use a scalpel for fine cutting and trimming work.

Measuring jug: The 500 ml (1 pint/2 cup) is most useful.

Modelling tools: These may be bought from specialist suppliers although you will be able to improvise with various common household tools.

Moulds: Used in sugarcraft and chocolate work and come in a wide variety of shapes and sizes for many different occasions.

1   *Rolling pin and worksurface.*
2   *Greaseproof (waxed) paper.*
3   *Metal modelling tools.*
4   *Scissors.*
5   *Garrett frill cutter.*
6   *Smoothers.*
7   *Crimpers.*
8   *Selection of pastry and biscuit cutters.*
9   *Kitchen knife.*
10   *Palette knives.*
11   *Paste colours.*
12   *Sugarcraft pens.*
13   *Small non-stick rolling pin and board.*
14   *Wooden modelling tools.*
15   *Paintbrushes.*
16   *Florist's wire and wire cutters.*
17   *Flower cutters.*
18   *Piping tubes.*
19   *Petal dust.*
20   *Cake boards and cards.*

Palette knife: Crank-handled and straight palette knives are used for lifting, smoothing and trimming.

Paper and card: Greaseproof (waxed) and silicone paper is used for icing bags and runouts. Card is used to make templates.

Piping bag stand: Not essential but keeps the worksurface clean and stops the tubes, once filled from drying out.

Piping tubes: Various sizes and shapes are available in both nickel plate and plastic. The former are more expensive but tend to be more accurate and defined.

Rolling pin: An extra long or non-stick pin is necessary and a smaller stainless steel or non-stick pin is useful for making plaques and for fine work.

Scissors: One good pair of large scissors and a pair of sharp fine-bladed scissors are also required.

Scrapers: Plain and serrated plastic side scrapers are used for putting icing on the sides of cakes.

Scriber: Fine lines are scratched or scribed onto the cake using a scriber.

Sieve: Keep a small fine mesh sieve for sieving icing (confectioner's) sugar only.

Smoothers: These are used to smooth the surface of marzipanned or sugarpasted cakes although some people prefer to use their hands.

Spacers: These help to maintain uniform thickness when rolling out sugarpaste or marzipan.

Spatula: Plastic or rubber for use in cake and icing preparation and wooden for mixing royal icing.

Straight edge: Used when flat icing the top of a cake with royal icing.

Tweezers: Fine pointed tweezers with grooved ends.

Turntable: Preferably a quality turntable; a tilting one is best for some jobs.

Wooden dowelling: Used for pulled flower work and modelling.

Worksurface: Melamine, non-stick plastic, marble or wooden surfaces are best. Be sure that they are thoroughly clean and grease-free.

Care of Equipment: Wash each piece of equipment thoroughly after use in warm, mild detergent taking care to ensure that all items are free of grease. Rinse before drying. Store in a dry, dust-free environment, rewash before use if necessary.

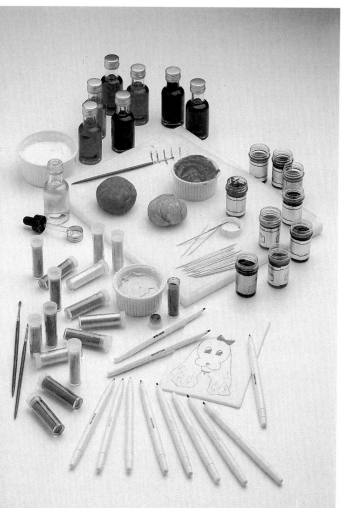

FOOD COLOURING

Food colouring comes in four main forms: powders, liquid, paste and pens.

Powder is mainly used as petal dust for adding colour to flowers and frills. It can be used to colour the icing itself but the intensity is not so strong as with paste or liquid colouring so it is uneconomical to use in large quantities. However, it should be used for lace and filigree work as paste contains glycerine and liquid would make the icing too soft for fine work. Powders should also be used when colouring white chocoate as other types would cause it to thicken.

Liquid colourings are readily available but are less concentrated than pastes consequently making sugarpaste more sticky and royal icing too soft if used in any quantity. Use for pastel shades only and use paste for dark colours.

Paste colours are generally the best to use for colouring royal icing or sugarpaste. Pastes are glycerine based and come in a good colour range. Use a cocktail stick to add the colour to the icing and use sparingly.

Sugarcraft pens are also available and are used for marking outlines, and writing on surfaces. They are used like a felt pen.

CRIMPERS

The plaque shows a full set of crimpers with their corresponding effects. Crimping is a quick and versatile method of decoration for marzipanned and sugarpasted surfaces. Crimping must always be worked on soft paste so is generally worked as soon as the cake is covered. When using crimpers dip in cornflour (cornstarch) to prevent them sticking to the paste while working. Pinch the crimper slightly so the edges are about 5 mm (¼ in) from the closed position, place on the sugarpaste surface and bring your thumb and first finger together. Squeeze the crimper to create the desired effect.

The numbers along the edge of the plaque relate to the particular set of crimpers shown here.

No 1	Single open scallop	No 6	Chevron
No 2	Single closed scallop	No 7	Straight edge
No 3	Double open scallop	No 8	Heart
No 4	Double closed scallop	No 9	Holly
No 5	Diamond		

CAKE BOARDS

The board that you choose does not always have to be the same shape as the cake, for instance, a round cake can look attractive on a petal-shaped board. It all depends on the effect that you want to achieve. Most of the unusual cake boards come in three or four sizes to match the size of the tins (pans).

The basic guideline for the size of board is that the board should be 5 cm (2 in) larger than the cake. The bottom tier of a wedding cake or any cake with a collar should have a board 7.5 cm (3 in) larger. On wedding cakes it is important not to overshadow the cakes, so the chosen board should not be larger than the cake that is on the tier below.

Some manufacturers still make boards to the imperial standard thickness of a half inch. Metric boards are slightly thicker at 2 cm. When making a tiered cake, be sure to use boards of the same thickness throughout. If the boards are to be trimmed with ribbons, these should also be of the same width.

Fruit cakes should always go on 2 cm (¾ in) thick drum cake boards or wooden boards to take the weight of the cake. The other boards, known as double-thick cards are only suitable for sponge or novelty cakes.

Specialist shops stock a wide variety of cake boards to complement the various cake tins (pans); they are often available by mail order.

BANDING CAKE BOARDS

Any kind of ribbon can be used to trim the cake board. Choose colours which combine or contrast with the colours of the cake. It is usual to pin the ribbons onto the board; do not use glue, which may stain the ribbon or give off toxic fumes.

Hold the board firmly and use a long, flat-headed pin to attach the ribbon in position. Stretch the ribbon tightly around the board. If the board is large it may be necessary to use more pins or dabs of royal icing to keep the ribbon from slipping. Pin in place at the join. Cut the ribbon evenly.

If adding a contrasting band, pin over the join and stretch the ribbon around the board as for the first one. Pin the second ribbon and trim neatly. Finish off the board by pinning a small bow over the join.

CAKE STANDS AND ACCESSORIES

There are a great many styles of cake stand available for purchase or for hire. They range from the very elaborate to the plain and simple and it is important to choose one that fits in with the style and colour scheme of your cake. Some multi-tiered stands are now available, these enable you to place two or even three cakes on one stand without the use of pillars and look particularly good with a modern-style wedding cake. In addition to the stands, matching knives add a finishing touch to a wedding cake especially if they are decorated with flowers and ribbons to match the cake.

PILLARS

The traditional white, silver or gold pillars are still the best type of pillar for a highly decorated, classic cake but there are several styles of perspex (plexiglass) pillars available which look excellent on a cake which has a contemporary design.

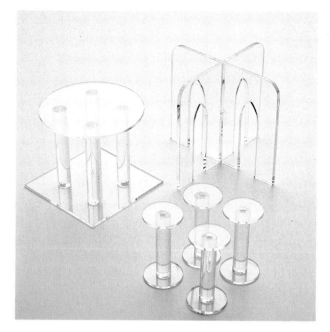

15

DESIGNING A CAKE

When designing a cake, the first thing to consider is for what occasion the cake is to be used. If decorating a cake for a children's party or for elderly people, it is best to avoid any decoration that is not edible.

The next thing to think of is the number of people the cake must serve. This will determine the size of the cake and the number of tiers. There may be occasions when people want a small, tiered wedding cake. In this case, all decorations have to be reduced in size. A small cake will be overwhelmed by large flowers, so everything must be miniaturized.

The next decision is about colour: which colours will combine best with the overall design. Get colour samples or fresh flowers to work from, particularly if strong colours are to be used.

Consider the proportions and balance of the design. There are many books describing the rules and regulations for this. However, fashion does change, and ideas with it. The best guide is your eye, together with these few basic guidelines.

Traditionally, royal-iced cakes have a graduation of 5 cm (2 in) between tiers, and it has also been traditional that the depth of the top tier is less than that of the bottom tier. However, if a cake is covered in sugarpaste, it is usual to have a 7.5 cm (3 in) differential in tier size, and for the depth of all the tiers to be the same. If supporting the tiers with pillars, those on a royal-iced cake can decrease in height, while pillars on a sugarpasted cake must be the same height.

The board for the lowest tier of a cake can be proportionately larger than the boards of the upper tiers. The boards in a tiered cake should be the same size as the cake in the layer immediately below. If using a vase of sugar flowers on the top of a cake, have the tiers graduated in 5 cm (2 in) sizes. This creates a more attractively proportioned cake than the usual 7.5 cm (3 in) graduations.

Detail of the top tier of the wedding cake shown with a different top arrangement.

When designing a tiered cake with embroidery and lace, keep in mind the depths of the cakes. If decreasing the depth of each tier, the lace and embroidery designs must be decreased in the same proportions or the designs will look very heavy on the smallest tier. When designing scallops for a three-tier cake, it is easier to match a design by dividing it into three when starting to work.

Before beginning to decorate a cake, have a mental picture of what it should look like when finished. Draw it so that you have something to refer to while decorating. Remember, though, that sometimes when working on a cake a different pattern may start to emerge. If it looks good, follow it, even if it is not the design originally planned. Instinct plays a great part in creativity, and new ideas are continually being sought by enthusiastic cake decorators.

PEACH AND WHITE WEDDING CAKE
This perfectly designed three-tiered cake incorporates a simple piped rose motif with delicate lace work. The ribbon trim and tiny bows at each corner pick up the peach colour and complete the design. Silk roses, blossom and gypsophila combined with thin ribbons make up the posies on the bottom two cakes and the arrangement on the top tier.

SPONGE CAKES

A plain or flavoured sponge cake makes the perfect vehicle for many decorative techniques. There are several recipes given in this chapter including a basic sponge cake ideal for buttercream and other soft icings and the firmer Madeira cake which can be coated with sugarpaste. The ingredients are given in chart form so that you can be certain that you are making the correct amount of cake mixture for your requirement.

The featured cakes are all sponges which are cut into various animal shapes and then decorated to make wonderful children's birthday cakes. No real decorating skills are employed, just a little imagination and a sense of fun.

SPONGE CAKES

PREPARING THE TIN (PAN)

For all cakes, good preparation of the tin (pan) is essential.

Place the tin (pan) over a piece of greaseproof (waxed) paper. Use a pencil to draw around the outside of the tin. Cut out the marked shape using a pair of sharp scissors.

Brush the tin (pan) lightly with oil and fit the greaseproof (waxed) paper disc over the base of the tin. Brush the paper with oil.

BASIC SPONGE CAKE

This is a traditional sponge cake made by creaming together the butter and sugar to incorporate the air. Different flavourings can be added to give variety. The mixture may be cooked in many different tin (pan) shapes and sizes (see chart).

Place butter or margarine and sugar in a mixing bowl. Mix together with a wooden spoon, then beat for 2–3 minutes until light and fluffy. Alternatively, use an electric mixer for about 1 minute.

Add eggs a little at a time, beating well after each addition, until all the egg has been incorporated and the mixture is soft and glossy. If it looks slightly curdled, beat in 15–30 ml (1–2 tablespoons) of flour.

Sift flour and baking powder into bowl and add flavourings if desired. Using a spatula or a large spoon, carefully fold in flour, cutting through and turning the mixture until all the flour has been incorporated into batter.

Place mixture in the prepared greased and lined tin (pan), smooth top with a spatula and give the tin a sharp tap to remove any air pockets and to level the top.

Place cake in the centre of a preheated oven 160C (325F/Gas 3) for specified cooking time (see chart). Test cake by pressing centre with the fingers, it should be golden brown and feel firm and springy when cooked.

Loosen edges with palette knife, invert onto cooling rack and remove lining paper. Turn cake the right way up and leave until completely cold.

VARIATIONS

Flavourings for a 2-egg quantity of Basic Sponge Cake (increase the amounts for larger quantities of cake mixture):

15 ml (3 teaspoons) cocoa blended with 15 ml (3 tablespoons) boiling water

10 ml (2 teaspoons) instant coffee blended with 5 ml (1 teaspoon) boiling water

5–10 ml (1–2 teaspoons) finely grated orange, lemon or lime rind

2.5 ml (½ teaspoon) vanilla, almond or peppermint esence (extract)

25 g (1 oz/3 teaspoons) chocolate dots (chips) or grated chocolate

50 g (2 oz/¼ Cup) glacé (candied) cherries, chopped

BASIC SPONGE CHART

Tin (pan) sizes	18 cm (7 in) shallow square tin 20 cm (8 in) round sandwich (shallow) tin	1 kg (2 lb) loaf tin 23 cm (9 in) ring mould (tube pan)	940 ml (30 fl oz/3¾ Cups) pudding basin (bowl) or mould	Two 18 cm (7 in) shallow square tins Two 20 cm (8 in) sandwich (shallow) tins	1 litre (32 fl oz/4 Cups) pudding basin (bowl) 18 cm (7 in) mould	1 kg (2 lb) loaf tin 28 cm x 18 cm (1 in x 7 in) mould	Two 20 cm (8 in) round sandwich (shallow) tins Two 23 cm (9 in) round sandwich (shallow) tins	23 cm (9 in) deep round or square cake tin
Soft butter margarine	125 g (4 oz/½ Cup)	125 g (4 oz/½ Cup)	125 g (4 oz/½ Cup)	185 g (6 oz/¾ Cup)	185 g (6 oz/¾ Cup)	185 g (6 oz/¾ Cup)	250 g (8 oz/1 Cup)	250 g (8 oz/1 Cup)
Caster (superfine) sugar	125 g (4 oz/½ Cup)	125 g (4 oz/½ Cup)	125 g (4 oz/½ Cup)	185 g (6 oz/¾ Cup)	185 g (6 oz/¾ Cup)	185 g (6 oz/¾ Cup)	250 g (8 oz/1 Cup)	250 g (8 oz/1 Cup)
Medium eggs	2	2	2	3	3	3	4	4
Self-raising flour	125 g (4 oz/1 Cup)	125 g (4 oz/1 Cup)	125 g (4 oz/1 Cup)	185 g (6 oz/1½ Cups)	185 g (6 oz/1½ Cups)	185 g (6 oz/1½ Cups)	250 g (8 oz/2 Cups)	250 g 8 oz/2 Cups)
Baking powder	5 ml (1 teaspoon)	5 ml (1 teaspoon)	5 ml (1 teaspoon)	7.5 ml (1½ teaspoons)	7.5 ml (1½ teaspoons)	7.5 ml (1½ teaspoons)	10 ml (2 teaspoons)	10 ml (2 teaspoons)
Approximate cooking time	35 to 40 minutes	30 to 35 minutes	50 to 55 minutes	30 to 35 minutes	60 to 70 minutes	45 to 55 minutes	35 to 40 minutes	55 to 65 minutes

QUICK MADEIRA CAKE

A good, plain cake which can be made as an alternative to a light or rich fruit cake. It is firm and moist and makes a good base for icing and decorating.

Place flour, baking powder, sugar, margarine, eggs and milk or juice into a mixing bowl. Mix together with a wooden spoon, then beat for 2–3 minutes until smooth and glossy. Alternatively, use an electric mixer and beat for 1 minute only. Add flavourings, if desired and mix until well blended.

Place mixture into prepared greased and lined tin (pan); smooth top with a spatula and give the tin a sharp tap to remove any air pockets and to level the top.

Place the cake in the centre of a preheated oven 160C (325F/Gas 3) for the specified cooking time (see chart). Test cake by pressing the centre with fingers. It should be golden brown, and feel springy when cooked.

Loosen edges with palette knife, invert onto a wire rack and remove lining paper. Turn cake the right way up and leave until completely cold.

VARIATIONS

Flavourings for a 3-egg quantity of Madeira Cake (increase the amounts for larger quantities of cake mixture):

Cherry: add 185 g (6 oz/1 Cup) glacé (candied) cherries, halved

Coconut: add 60 g (2 oz/⅔ Cup) desiccated (shredded) coconut

Nut: replace 125 g (4 oz/1 Cup) flour with ground almonds, hazelnuts, walnuts or pecan nuts

Citrus: replace milk with lemon, orange or lime juice and 5 ml (1 teaspoon) of grated lemon, orange or lime rind

AMERICAN SPONGE CAKE

This white sponge cake makes a good base for a celebration cake; it can be marzipanned, iced and decorated.

125 g (4 oz/½ Cup) butter, softened
185 g (6 oz/¾ Cup) caster (superfine) sugar
220 g (7 oz/1¾ Cups) plain (all-purpose) flour
10 ml (2 teaspoons) baking powder
125 ml (4 fl oz/½ Cup) water
2.5 ml (½ teaspoon) vanilla essence (extract)
4 medium egg whites
Cake tin (pan) sizes 18 cm square, 20 cm (8 in) round, 23 cm (9 in) ring (tube)

Place butter and sugar in a mixing bowl. Mix together with a wooden spoon, then beat for 2–3 minutes until light and fluffy. Alternatively, use an electric mixer for 1 minute.

Sift together flour and baking powder. Gradually add to the mixture with water, beating well after each addition, until all the flour and water have been incorporated, to form a smooth lump-free batter. Stir in vanilla.

Place egg whites in a clean, grease-free bowl and whisk until stiff, but not dry. Add one-third of the egg white to the mixture. Using a spatula or large metal spoon, carefully fold in egg white, cutting through and turning mixture until all the egg white has been incorporated. Repeat the process with remaining egg white.

Pour mixture into the prepared greased and lined tin (pan) and gently level top with spatula. Place the cake into the centre of a preheated oven 180C (350F/Gas 4) for 35–45 minutes. Test the cake by pressing the centre with the fingers, it should be golden brown and feel firm and springy when cooked.

Loosen the edges with a palette knife and invert onto a wire rack. Carefully remove lining paper, turn cake the right way up and leave until cold.

QUICK MADEIRA CHART

Tin (pan) sizes	15 cm (6 in) square 18 cm (7 in) round	18 cm (7 in) square 20 cm (8 in) round	20 cm (8 in) square 23 cm (9 in) round	23 cm (9 in) square 25 cm (10 in) round
Plain (all-purpose) flour	250 g (8 oz/2 Cups)	375 g (12 oz/3 Cups)	500 g (1 lb/4 Cups)	560 g (1 lb 2 oz/4½ Cups)
Baking powder	5 ml (1 teaspoon)	7.5 ml (1½ teaspoons)	10 ml (2 teaspoons)	12.5 ml (2½ teaspoons)
Caster (superfine) sugar	185 g (6 oz/¾ Cup)	315 g (10 oz/1¼ Cups)	440 g (14 oz/1¾ Cups)	500 g (1 lb/2 Cups)
Soft margarine	185 g (6 oz/¾ Cup)	315 g (10 oz/1¼ Cups)	440 g (14 oz/1¾ Cups)	500 g (1 lb/2 Cups)
Medium eggs	3	5	7	8
Milk or citrus juice	30 ml (6 teaspoons)	45 ml (9 teaspoons)	52.5 ml (10 teaspoons)	60 ml (2 fl oz/¼ Cup)
Approximate cooking time	1¼–1½ hours	1½–1¾ hours	1¾–2 hours	1¾–2 hours

GENOESE SPONGE CAKE

A rich sponge cake made with melted butter which gives a moist, light texture. It will cut well into different shapes for small, large or novelty cakes, and it is easy to ice.

4 medium eggs
125 g (4 oz/½ Cup) caster (superfine) sugar
125 g (4 oz/1 Cup) plain (all-purpose) flour
60 g (2 oz/¼ Cup) unsalted (sweet) butter, melted
Cake tin (pan) sizes 33 cm x 23 cm (13 in x 9 in), two 18 cm (7 in) square, two 20 cm (8 in) round sandwich (shallow)

Place eggs and sugar in heatproof bowl. Place bowl over a saucepan of hot, but not boiling water and whisk immediately. Whisk until thick and pale, 3 – 4 minutes. Remove bowl from saucepan and continue whisking until mixture leaves a trail on the surface when whisk is lifted.

Sift flour onto surface of mixture and add flavourings, if desired. Pour melted butter around the edge of mixture.

Using a spatula or large spoon, carefully fold in flour and butter, cutting through and turning mixture gently until all the flour has been incorporated.

Pour mixture into the prepared greased and lined tin (pan) and gently level top with spatula. Place cake in the centre of a preheated oven 180C (350F/Gas 4) for 15 – 20 minutes. Test the cake by pressing centre with fingers, it should be golden brown and feel firm and springy when cooked.

Loosen the edges with a palette knife and invert onto a wire rack. Carefully remove lining paper, turn cake the right way up and leave until completely cold.

VARIATIONS
Chocolate: replace 30 g (1 oz/¼ Cup) flour with cocoa powder
Coffee: add 20 ml (4 teaspoons) instant coffee powder to the flour
Citrus: add 10 ml (2 teaspoons) grated orange, lemon or lime rind
Nut: replace 60 g (2 oz/½ Cup) flour with finely ground nuts

WHISKED SPONGE CAKE

A light, fat-free sponge suitable for making into Swiss (jelly) rolls, small and large iced and decorated sponge and novelty cakes.

2 medium eggs
60 g (2 oz/¼ Cup) caster (superfine) sugar
60 g (2 oz/½ Cup) plain (all-purpose) flour
2.5 ml (½ teaspoon) baking powder
Cake tin (pan) sizes 28 cm x 18 cm (11 in x 7 in) Swiss (jelly) roll tin, 18 cm (7 in) shallow square, 20 cm (8 in) round sandwich (shallow)

Place eggs and sugar in a heatproof bowl over a saucepan of hot but not boiling water. Whisk the mixture until thick and pale. Remove the bowl from saucepan and continue whisking until whisk leaves a trail on the surface when lifted.

Sift flour and baking powder onto surface of the mixture and add flavourings if desired. Using a spatula or a large spoon, carefully fold in flour, cutting through and turning the mixture until all the flour has been incorporated.

Pour mixture into prepared greased and lined tin (pan) and gently level top with spatula. Place cake in the centre of a preheated oven 180C (350F/Gas 4) for 10 – 15 minutes for Swiss (jelly) roll or 15 – 20 minutes for square or round cakes. Test the cake by

As well as round and square tins (pans), there are a great many unusually shaped and novelty tins available.

pressing the centre with the fingers, it should be golden brown and feel firm and springy when cooked.

Loosen edges with a palette knife and invert onto a wire rack. Carefully remove the lining paper, turn the cake the right way up and leave until cold.

VARIATIONS

Chocolate: replace 15 g (½ oz/6 teaspoons) flour with cocoa powder

Coffee: add 10 ml (2 teaspoons) instant coffee powder to the flour

Citrus: add 5 ml (1 teaspoon) grated orange, lemon or lime rind

Nut: replace 30 g (1 oz/¼ Cup) flour with finely ground nuts

Trim 5 mm (¼ in) off each side of the cake using a sharp knife.

Spread the trimmed cake evenly with warmed apricot jam.

MAKING A SWISS ROLL

Make a Swiss (jelly) roll as described for whisked sponge cake using a Swiss (jelly) roll tin (pan).

Invert the cooked cake onto sugared paper then carefully peel off the lining paper.

Roll the cake towards you into a firm roll starting with the aid of the paper, from the short edge.

SIMPLE DECORATIONS

There are many simple ways in which a basic sponge cake can be decorated without spending a lot of time. It is always a pleasure to add a finishing touch to a cake to turn it into something a little more special.

Icing (confectioner's) sugar is one ingredient which, when used carefully, can transform the appearance of a cake. Simply dredging the surface with icing (confectioner's) sugar makes a sponge cake more appealing. Try placing a patterned doily on top of a cake, or arranging 1 cm (½ in) strips of paper in lines or a lattice pattern on top of the cake; then dredge with icing (confectioner's) sugar. Carefully remove the doily or paper, to reveal the pattern. This looks effective on a chocolate or coffee cake.

Fruit rinds cut into fine shreds, or shapes using tiny cutters, make an effective edible decoration. Cut thin strips of lemon, orange or lime rind from the fruits, taking care not to include the white pith. For shreds, use a sharp knife to cut the rind into narrow lengths and use to sprinkle over piped cream (see Swiss roll on cover). Using tiny aspic cutters, cut out various shapes. Arrange these shapes on glacé icing or cakes iced with buttercream to form flowers, stems and leaves, or just as a border using different coloured rinds.

DECORATIONS WITH FLOWERS

Flowers seem a natural decoration to go on a cake, however, it is important to check that they are edible. Tiny fresh flowers positioned at the last minute look so pretty. Also attractive are sugar-frosted flowers, which are preserved with egg white and sugar; they will last for several weeks once they are dry.

To sugar-frost flowers, ensure they are fresh and dry and trim the stems to the length required. Pull the petals apart if you wish to frost each one of them separately.

Place some caster (superfine) sugar in a shallow bowl. Using a fine paint brush, paint each petal on both sides with egg white which has been lightly beaten. Brush the centre and stem, then carefully spoon over the sugar to coat evenly.

Place the flowers on a cooling rack covered with kitchen paper and leave in a warm, dry place until the flowers are completely dry and set hard.

Store in a box lined with kitchen paper for up to three weeks.

PURCHASED DECORATIONS

Purchased decorations are instant decorations, and chosen carefully, can make a pretty finish to a cake. Angelica can be cut into stems, leaves and diamond shapes. Glacé (candied) cherries in various colours can be cut in half or sliced into rings or into thin wedges and arranged as petal shapes for flowers. Sugar flowers, jelly diamonds (gumdrops), crystallized flower petals all make attractive decorations on top of icing swirls or as a border design. Coloured dragées, sugared mimosa balls, hundreds and thousands (sprinkles) and coloured sugar strands make quick, colourful coatings, toppings and designs. For children's cakes, sweets (candies) are always a favourite; white and chocolate buttons, coloured (jelly) beans and liquorice sweets can all be used for simple finishes.

RORY LION

3-egg quantity basic sponge mix baked in a 20 cm (8 in)
  round cake tin (pan)
Apricot jam (jelly)
225 g (8 oz) yellow marzipan
Royal icing
Brown, orange, yellow and red food colouring
2 mint sweets (candies)
2 chocolate drops or beans
Few pieces wholewheat spaghetti

Make up the sponge mix and divide between three
bowls. Leave one plain and colour one yellow and
one orange. Put the mixture into the tin in spoonfuls,
alternating the colours. Mix gently together with the
handle of a fork or spoon to marble the mixture. Bake
according to recipe.

When cold, decorate the cake as follows. Spread
the top of the cake with sieved apricot jam (jelly).
Roll out 185 g (6 oz) of the marzipan and cut out
a 15 cm (6 in) circle, and two 5 cm (2 in) circles.
Place the large circle in the centre of the cake. Colour
a little of the remaining marzipan dark brown. From
this, cut out four 2.5 cm (1 in) circles and shape a
triangular nose. Put two of the dark brown circles
on to the two plain circles. Press lightly together and
pinch one side to make ears. Using a little royal icing,
attach the ears to the head.

Use the remaining dark brown circles, mints and
chocolate drops for eyes and attach with royal icing.
With a skewer, make nostrils in the nose. Attach to
cake with icing. Colour a tiny piece of marzipan red
and shape into a tongue. Roll remaining plain
marzipan into two balls and flatten slightly. Prick
them with a skewer and then attach with icing just
under the nose. Attach tongue.

Divide the royal icing between three bowls. Colour
one yellow, one orange and one brown. Using a large
piping bag fitted with a large star tube, put the three
icings side by side. Squeeze out into strips around
the lion's head to make a stripy mane. Blend in
lightly with a fork. Carefully push in spaghetti
whiskers.

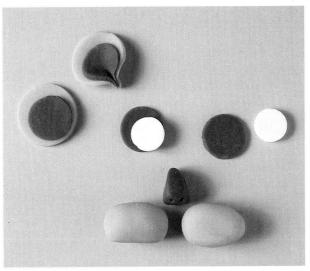

Marzipan shapes for face and shaping ears.

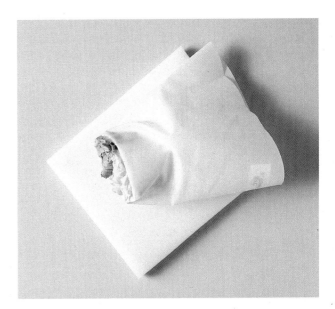

*Filling piping bag for multi-stripe piping (above) and
resulting effect (below).*

PRETTY KITTY CAKE

Two   20 cm (8 in) round sponge cakes
Buttercream icing made with 250 g (8 oz/1 cup) butter,
*   500 g (1 lb/3 cups) icing (confectioner's) sugar (see page*
*   54)*
Desiccated (shredded) coconut
Pink food colouring
Shoe lace liquorice
Chocolate bean or button
Glacé (candied) cherry
2 sweets (candies) for eyes
Ribbon, foil or crêpe paper for bow

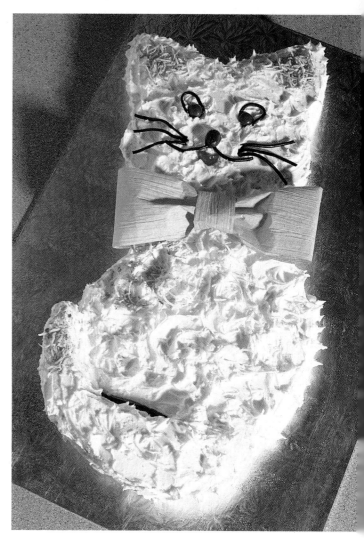

Cut the sponges as shown (page 248). Place the body
on a large cake board. Using a little buttercream,
attach the head to the body at a slight angle. Cut
the ears as shown and join with buttercream. Attach
to the head with buttercream. Cut the tail as shown.
Sandwich the two pieces together with buttercream.
Attach the broad end of tail to cat's bottom using
a little icing. Lift the end of the tail on to the cat's
body so it curls as shown. Use a little icing to fill
in the gaps and make smooth.

Cover the entire cake with remaining icing. Using
a palette knife, swirl the icing to look like fur. Colour
a little of the coconut pink and sprinkle on to the
ears, chest and tip of tail. Scatter a little white
coconut over the rest of the body. Use liquorice strips
for eyes, mouth and whiskers. Place a chocolate bean
for nose, sweets (candies) for eyes and cherry for
mouth. Put a ribbon or paper bow at kitty's neck.

Cutting of sponges.

Curling up of tail.

28

BUTTERFLY BEAUTY

Two 28 x 18 cm (11 x 7 in) oblong sponge cakes (2-egg
quantity each)
Buttercream icing made with 185 g (6 oz/¾ cup) butter,
375 g (12 oz/2 cups) icing (confectioner's) sugar (see page
54)
Pink or lilac food colouring
1 marshmallow cable
1 marshmallow
Approx 200 g (7 oz) sweets (candies)
Pipe cleaner

Cut the cakes (page 247). Place on a board, joining
the centres with a little buttercream. Remove one-
third of the icing and colour pale pink or lilac.
Remove 6 teaspoons of the coloured icing and colour
a deeper shade of pink or lilac. Spread the uncoloured
buttercream over the top of the cake around the
outside edge. Put the pale pink or lilac in the middle
and blend into the white using a palette knife. Put
the darkest colour in centre and blend as before.

Place the marshmallow cable down the centre to
represent the body. Stick on a marshmallow for the
head. Decorate the wings with sweets (candies).
Finally, bend a pipe cleaner into the shape of
antennae and push into head.

Cutting cake.

Blending icings.

FRUIT CAKES

The classic rich fruit cake is perfect for any occasion worthy of celebrating and the one given here is moist, laden with fruit and absolutely delicious. There is also a recipe for a lighter cake which still contains a substantial quantity of fruit but it is not so heavy and consequently does not keep so well as the rich cake.

These fruit cakes are, of course, perfect for marzipanning and coating with sugarpaste or royal icing but, if time is short, or the recipient of the cake is not keen on icing then maybe decorating with glacé (candied) fruit is the answer, it certainly looks very rich and splendid. Glacé fruit is expensive, but if you plan in advance you can make your own – it could even double as a gift in itself. Dried fruits and nuts may also be used with equal effect or the decoration can even be baked into the cake itself.

PREPARING A DEEP TIN

For rich cakes, use good quality fixed-based deep cake tins (pans). Ensure you have the correct-sized tin for the quantity of cake mixture as this will affect the depth and cooking time of the cake. Always measure the tin across the base, not the top.

Double-line the inside of the tin with greaseproof (waxed) or non-stick paper and the outside with double-thickness brown paper. Stand the tin on a baking sheet lined with 3 or 4 thicknesses of brown paper. This prevents the side and base of the cake from being overcooked.

Place the tin on double-thickness greaseproof or non-stick silicone baking paper and draw around the base. Cut out the shape with a pair of scissors.

Cut a strip of double-thickness greaseproof or non-stick paper long enough to wrap around the outside of the tin with a small overlap and to stand 2.5 cm (1 in) above the top of the tin.

Brush the base and sides of the tin with melted fat or oil. Place the cut-out shape in the base of the tin and smooth out the creases.

Place the double strip of paper inside the tin, pressing well against the sides and making sharp creases where it fits into corners.

Brush the base and side paper well with melted fat or oil. Place a double-thickness strip of brown paper around the outside of the tin and tie securely with string.

RICH FRUIT CAKE

This recipe makes a very moist, rich cake suitable for any celebration. The cake can be made in stages, if time is short or if you are making more than one cake.

The fruit may be prepared and soaked overnight and the cake made the following day. Once the mixture is in the tin (pan), the surface may be covered with plastic wrap and the cake stored in a cool place overnight if cooking is not possible on the day. The quantities have been carefully worked out so that the depth of each cake is the same. This is important when making tiers for a wedding cake, as they must all be the same depth.

In a large mixing bowl place the raisins, sultanas, currants, apricots, glacé (candied) cherries, mixed peel, nuts, lemon rind and juice, brandy, whisky or sherry. Mix all the ingredients together until well blended, then cover the bowl with plastic wrap. This mixture of fruit can be left overnight if required.

In another mixing bowl place the flour, mixed spice, ground almonds, sugar, butter, treacle and eggs. Mix together with a wooden spoon then beat for 2–3 minutes until smooth and glossy, or beat for 1–2 minutes using an electric mixer or food processor.

Place mixed fruit in bowl with cake mixture. Stir gently until all the fruit has been mixed into cake mixture.

Spoon mixture carefully into the prepared tin and spread evenly over the base and into the corners.

Pictures showing correct preparation of tins (pans).

Give the tin a few sharp taps to level the mixture and to remove any air pockets. Smooth the surface with the back of a metal spoon dipped in hot water, making a slight depression in the centre. The cake surface may be covered with plastic wrap and left overnight in a cool place if required.

Place cake in the centre of a pre-heated oven 140C (275F/Gas 1) for specified cooking time (see chart).

Test cake to see if it is cooked 15 minutes before the end of the cooking time. If cooked, the cake should feel firm, and a fine skewer or cocktail stick (toothpick) inserted into centre should come out quite clean. If cake is not cooked, re-test at 15 minute intervals. Allow to cool in tin.

Turn cake out of tin but do not remove lining papers as it helps to keep cake moist. Spoon over half quantity of brandy, whisky or sherry according to the quantities used in the chart, then wrap in double-thickness foil.

Store cake in a cool, dry place on its base with top uppermost for a week. Unwrap cake and spoon over remaining brandy, whisky or sherry (unless the cake is to be stored for three months in which case add the liquid a little at a time at monthly intervals). Re-wrap well and invert cake and store it upside down to keep the top flat. The cake will store for up to 3 months.

Cool the cooked cake in the tin (pan).

RICH FRUIT CAKE CHART

Tin (pan) size	13 cm (5 in) square 15 cm (6 in) round	18 cm (7 in) square 20 cm (8 in) round	23 cm (9 in) square 25 cm (10 in) round	28 cm (11 in) square 30 cm (12 in) round
Raisins	125 g (4 oz/⅔ Cup)	250 g (8 oz/1½ Cups)	375 g (12 oz/2¼ Cups)	560 g (1 lb 2 oz/3¼ Cups)
Sultanas	125 g (4 oz/⅔ Cup)	250 g (8 oz/1½ Cups)	375 g (12 oz/2¼ Cups)	560 g (1 lb 2 oz/3¼ Cups)
Currants	125 g (4 oz/⅔ Cup)	155 g (5 oz/1 Cup)	315 g (10 oz/2 Cups)	440 g (14 oz/2¾ Cups)
Dried apricots, chopped	60 g (2 oz/⅓ Cup)	125 g (4 oz/¾ Cup)	185 g (6 oz/1 Cup)	250 g (8 oz/1⅓ Cups)
Glacé (candied) cherries, quartered	90 g (3 oz/¾ Cup)	155 g (5 oz/1 Cup)	220 g (7 oz/1⅓ Cup)	280 g (9 oz/1¾ Cup)
Cut mixed peel	30 g (1 oz/9 teaspoons)	60 g (2 oz/⅓ Cup)	125 g (4 oz/¾ Cup)	250 g (8 oz/1½ Cups)
Mixed chopped nuts	30 g (1 oz/¼ Cup)	60 g (2 oz/½ Cup)	125 g (4 oz/1 Cup)	250 g (8 oz/2 Cups)
Lemon rind, coarsely grated	5 ml (1 teaspoon)	10 ml (2 teaspoons)	15 ml (3 teaspoons)	22.5 ml (1½ tablespoons)
Lemon juice	15 ml (3 teaspoons)	30 ml (2 tablespoons)	45 ml (3 tablespoons)	75 ml (4 tablespoons)
Brandy, whisky, sherry	15 ml (3 teaspoons)	45 ml (3 tablespoons)	75 ml (5 tablespoons)	105 ml (6–7 tablespoons)
Plain (all-purpose) flour	185 g (6 oz/1½ Cups)	280 g (9 oz/2¼ Cups)	470 g (15 oz/3¾ Cups)	685 g (1 lb 6 oz/5¼ Cups)
Ground mixed spice	5 ml (1 teaspoon)	15 ml (3 teaspoons)	22.5 ml (4½ teaspoons)	35 ml (7 teaspoons)
Ground almonds	30 g (1 oz/¼ Cup)	60 g (2 oz/½ Cup)	90 g (3 oz/¾ Cup)	155 g (5 oz/1¼ Cups)
Soft dark brown sugar	125 g (4 oz/½ Cup)	220 g (7 oz/¾ Cup)	410 g (13 oz/1⅔ Cups)	625 g (1¼ lbs/2½ Cups)
Butter or margarine, softened	125 g (4 oz/½ Cup)	220 g (7 oz/¾ Cup)	410 g (13 oz/1⅔ Cups)	625 g (1¼ lbs/2½ Cups)
Black treacle (molasses)	7.5 ml (1½ teaspoons)	22.5 ml (4 teaspoons)	37.5 ml (2½ tablespoons)	60 ml (4 tablespoons)
Medium eggs	2	4	7	9
Approx cooking time	2–2¼ hours	2½–2¾ hours	3½–3¾ hours	4¾–5 hours
Brandy, whisky, sherry (to moisten after cooking)	15 ml (3 teaspoons)	30 ml (2 tablespoons)	75 ml (5 tablespoons)	105 ml (7 tablespoons)

33

LIGHT FRUIT CAKE

This is a very light, moist fruit cake. As there is less fruit in the cake, it has a tendency to dome during cooking, so make a deep depression in the centre before putting in the oven. The cake will keep for up to 4 weeks.

750 g (1 ½ lb/4 ½ Cups) mixed dried fruit
125 g (4 oz/⅔ Cup) glacé (candied) cherries, quartered
90 g (3 oz/¾ Cup) flaked almonds
15 ml (3 teaspoons) orange rind, coarsely grated
45 ml (9 teaspoons) orange juice
45 ml (9 teaspoons) sherry
500 g (1 lb/4 Cups) plain (all-purpose) flour
15 ml (3 teaspoons) ground mixed spice
440 g (14 oz/1 ¾ Cups) soft light brown sugar
440 g (14 oz/1 ¾ Cups) butter or margarine, softened
5 medium eggs
Cake tin (pan) sizes 20 cm (8 in) square, 23 cm (9 in) round

Place in a large mixing bowl mixed dried fruit, cherries, almonds, orange rind, orange juice and sherry. Mix all the ingredients together until well blended.

In another mixing bowl, combine flour, mixed spice, sugar, butter or margarine and eggs. Mix together with a wooden spoon until smooth and glossy, or beat for 1–2 minutes with an electric mixer or food processor.

Place mixed fruit in bowl with cake mixture, stir gently until fruit has been mixed evenly into cake mixture.

Spoon mixture into prepared cake tin (pan) and spread evenly over the base and into corners. Give tin a few sharp taps to level the mixture and remove any air pockets. Smooth surface with back of a metal spoon, making a fairly deep depression in centre.

Bake in a preheated oven 140C (275F/Gas 1) for 3 ¼ – 3 ¾ hours. Test the cake 15 minutes before the end of cooking time. If cooked, a fine skewer inserted into centre of cake will come out clean. If cake is not cooked, re-test at 15 minute intervals.

Leave to cool in tin, turn out but leave lining paper on to keep cake moist. Wrap in foil and store in a cool place for up to 4 weeks.

Light fruit cake.

GLACÉ (CANDIED) FRUIT CAKE

This recipe makes a light-coloured cake with a moist texture which is due to the addition of ground almonds to the mixture. The cake will store well for several weeks.

375 g (12 oz/3 Cups) plain (all-purpose) flour
5 ml (1 teaspoon) baking powder
185 g (6 oz/1 ⅔ Cups) ground almonds
375 g (12 oz/1 ½ Cups) caster (superfine) sugar
375 g (12 oz/1 ½ Cups) butter, softened
4 large eggs
375 g (12 oz/2 ¼ Cups) chopped mixed glacé (candied) fruits
125 g (4 oz/1 Cup) chopped Brazil nuts
Cake tin (pan) sizes 20 cm (8 in) square, 23 cm (9 in) round

Sift flour and baking powder into a bowl, add ground almonds, sugar, butter and eggs. Mix together with a wooden spoon and beat for 2–3 minutes until smooth and glossy, or beat for 1–2 minutes using an electric mixer or food processor.

Add fruit and nuts to the mixture and stir gently until well mixed. Spoon mixture into prepared tin (pan) and spread evenly over base and into corners. Give a few sharp taps to level mixture and make a slight depression in centre of cake.

Bake in the centre of a preheated oven 140C (275F/Gas 1) for 2 ¼ to 2 ½ hours. Test the cake by pressing centre with the fingers, it should feel firm and springy when cooked. Leave to cool in tin, then turn out and wrap in foil and store in a cool place for up to one week before decorating.

WHEATEN FRUIT CAKE

This wholesome fruit cake is made from a mixture of dried fruits, honey and wholewheat flour. It is easy to make and produces a moist cake which will keep for several weeks. Decorate it with fruit and nuts or cover it with marzipan and icing.

125 g (4 oz/½ Cup) butter
60 ml (2 fl oz/¼ Cup) clear honey
250 ml (8 fl oz/1 Cup) orange juice
375 g (12 oz/3 Cups) chopped dried apricots
250 g (8 oz/1½ Cups) chopped dried figs
250 g (8 oz/1½ Cups) chopped stoned dates
315 g (10 oz/2 Cups) raisins
375 g (12 oz/3 Cups) 85% wholewheat plain flour
10 ml (2 teaspoons) ground mixed spice
2 medium eggs, beaten
4 ml (¾ teaspoon) bicarbonate of soda (baking soda)
Cake tin (pan) sizes 18 cm (7 in) square, 20 cm (8 in) round

Place butter, honey and orange juice in a large saucepan. Heat gently until butter has melted, then bring to the boil. Remove saucepan from heat then stir in all the fruit until well mixed and leave until lukewarm.

Place flour, mixed spice and eggs in a large mixing bowl. Stir bicarbonate of soda quickly into fruit mixture, then add to flour mixture in bowl.

Mix together with a wooden spoon, then stir until well mixed. Spoon mixture into prepared tin (pan) and spread evenly over base and into corners. Give a few sharp taps to level mixture and make a slight depression in the centre.

Bake in the centre of a preheated oven 140C (275F/Gas 1) for about 2 hours. Test cake 15 minutes before end of cooking time. When cooked, a fine skewer or cocktail stick (toothpick) inserted into the centre of cake will come out clean. If the cake is not cooked, re-test at 15 minute intervals. leave to cool in tin then turn out and wrap in foil for up to 2 weeks.

STORING FRUIT CAKES

Leave the lining paper on the cakes, then wrap in a double layer of foil, waxed or greaseproof paper, and store in a cool, dry place. Never seal a cake in an airtight container as this may encourage mould growth.

Rich fruit cakes keep well, although they are moist, full of flavour and at their best when first made. The cakes do mature with keeping, but all fruit cakes are best eaten within 3 months. If you are going to keep a fruit cake for several months, pour on the alcohol a little at a time at monthly intervals, turning the cake each time.

Light fruit cakes are stored in the same way as rich fruit cakes, but as they contain less fruit, their keeping qualities are not so good. These cakes are at their best when first made, or within one month of baking.

Once the cakes have been marzipanned and iced they must be stored in cardboard boxes, to keep them dust-free, and left in a warm, dry atmosphere. Avoid damp and cold conditions as they cause the icing to stain and colourings to run.

Servings: Working out the number of servings from a round or square cake is extremely simple. It depends if you require just a small finger of cake, or a more substantial slice. Whether the cake is round or square, cut across the cake from edge to edge into about 2.5 cm (1 in) slices, or thinner if desired. Then cut each slice into 4 cm (1½ in) pieces, or to the size you require. It is then easy to calculate the number of cake slices you can cut from the cake. A square cake is larger than a round cake of the same size, and will yield more slices. On a round cake the slices become smaller at the curved edges, so keep this in mind when calculating the servings.

Wrap the cake, with the lining paper on, in foil ready to store.

CRYSTALLIZED AND GLACÉ (CANDIED) FRUITS

Crystallized and glacé (candied) fruits look lovely on fruit cakes and gâteaux, but they can be difficult to find and somewhat expensive. However, homemade fruits are easy to make requiring just a few minutes attention each day – the entire procedure takes 12 – 14 days.

It is possible to crystallize fresh fruits but canned fruit tends to be more successful as the preliminary processing makes it easier to handle. Pineapple, apricots, pears and lychees are particularly successful as they have a fairly firm texture to begin with. Orange and lemon slices can be prepared as for canned fruit.

Day 1:   choose fruit in syrup, drain and measure the syrup and make up 315 ml (10 fl oz/1 1/4 Cups) with hot water. Add 250 g (8 oz/1 Cup) sugar and add to the liquid. Use just sugar and water for the lemon or orange slices. Heat slowly in a pan until the sugar has melted then bring to the boil. Pour over the fruit, cover and leave for 24 hours. Repeat the procedure for each fruit type being crystallized – do not mix fruits.

Day 2:   drain the syrup from the fruit and add 60 g (2 oz/¼ Cup) sugar. Heat through gently until the sugar has dissolved, then bring to the boil and pour over fruit. Leave for 24 hours.

Crystallized fruit left to soak in a sugar syrup.

Days 3 and 4:   as day 2.

Day 5:   drain the syrup from the fruit and add 90 g (3 oz/⅓ Cup) sugar. Heat through gently until dissolved, then add the fruit, simmer for 4 minutes. Return to the bowl and soak for 48 hours.

Day 6   soaking.

Day 7:   as day 5.

Day 8 – 10:   soaking.

Day 11:   drain the fruit and place on wire racks placing a tray underneath to catch the drips. Place in a warm place such as the airing cupboard and leave for 2 – 3 days until dry, the fruit should feel barely sticky to touch. The process may be accelerated by drying the fruit in a very cool oven 50C (120F/Gas low) which takes about 24 hours.

When the fruit is dry, finish by rolling caster (superfine) sugar or with a glacé glaze. Use leftover syrups as a dessert sauce served over icecream, sponge puddings or flans.

Glacé glace: dissolve 500 g (1 lb/2 Cups) sugar into 185 ml (6 fl oz/¾ Cup) water. Bring to the boil and cover tightly with a lid to prevent further evaporation. Have a bowl of boiling water to hand as well as a cup of syrup, cocktail sticks (toothpicks) and some absorbent paper. Dip the fruit into the boiling water for 20 seconds, drain, then holding the fruit with the cocktail stick, dip the fruit quickly into the syrup and place on a wire rack. Repeat with remaining fruit discarding the syrup when it becomes cloudy. Dry as for crystallized fruit.

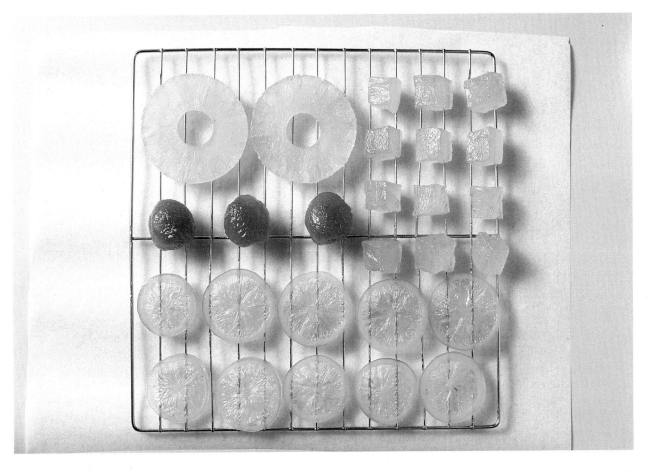

Once impregnated with sugar the fruit is left to dry out.   *Crystallized pineapple rolled in sugar and presented as a gift.*

JEWELLED FRUIT CAKE

20 cm (8 in) square rich or glacé fruit cake
Sieved apricot jam (jelly)
Aassortment of crystallized or glacé (candied) fruit (eg tangerines, black cherries, figs, red cherries, pineapple, strawberries, ginger)
Approximately 20 hazelnuts
1 metre (1 yd) 1 cm (½ in) wide gift wrap ribbon

Flatten the top of the cake if necessary by cutting with a sharp knife. Brush a generous layer of apricot jam (jelly) over the top of the cake. Lay a line of similarly sized and shaped hazelnuts across the cake diagonally from one corner to another. Either side of this line lay a row of sliced tangerines, black cherries, figs, strawberries, pineapple, red cherries and ginger. Reheat the apricot jam (jelly) and use to glaze and seal the surface of the cake. Place plain ribbon band round the cake.

VARIATION

Replace the hazelnuts with pecan nuts or almonds and arrange fruits of your choice on top of the cake.

CHERRY-ALMOND FLOWER CAKE

Uncooked 20 cm (8 in) round light fruit cake
4 cherry halves
20 blanched almonds
Angelica
1 metre (1 yd) 1 cm (½ in) wide gift-wrap ribbon

Make the mixture for the light fruit cake as directed and place in a prepared tin (pan). Using the back of a wooden spoon make quite a definite dip in the centre of the cake as it tends to rise in the centre. Arrange the cherries, almonds and angelica in the flower and leaf arrangement as seen on the cake. Do not worry if the almonds appear to be tipping backwards into the dip as they will straighten up as the cake rises. Bake the cake as normal but check after about 45 minutes to ensure that the decorations are not sinking, if they do look as if they might sink then carefully ease upwards with a cocktail stick. If using the specified recipe you should not run into this problem.

Alternative arrangements of fruit and nuts could be made in the same way. Concentric circles of various nuts and cherries look attractive or the entire surface could be covered with almonds as for a Dundee Cake or completely covered with cherries. For a more subtle appearance choose cherries dyed with natural colourings rather than with synthetic red. Finish the cake with simple ribbon band secured with a glass-headed pin.

MINIATURE FRUIT CAKES

The crystallized fruit designs on these small cakes are simple and highly adaptable. The cakes would make an ideal Christmas gift for a grandparent.

25 cm (10 in) square fruit cake
Sieved apricot jam (jelly)
Dried apricots
Dried dates
Glacé (candied) cherries (assorted colours)
Pecan nuts
Blanched almonds
Walnuts
Hazelnuts
Reel of curling gift wrap ribbon
Foiled gift wrap paper
Card

Cut the cake into nine equal-sized miniature cakes. Glaze the tops with apricot jam (jelly). Arrange the fruit and nuts attractively in diagonal lines across the cakes. Alternatively, pick out the recipient's initial in blanched almonds and create a decorative border of fruit and nuts.

Reheat the apricot jam and brush the tops generously to glaze and seal.

Make bows with long curling ends from the curling ribbon. Place ribbon around the cake and attach the ribbon using a glass-headed pin. To make the boards, cut squares of firm card, cut squares of gift-wrap paper about 5 cm (2 in) larger than the card. Cover the paper with glue or spray mount and attach to the card. Finish the back with parcel corners.

MARZIPAN

Homemade marzipan really does taste better than bought marzipan although with many white marzipans on the market now the quality and appearance of the latter are improving. Marzipan can be used as a base for royal icing or sugarpaste or can be the sole decoration on the cake. It lends itself well to colouring, crimping, cutout work and modelling so there really are endless designs that can be achieved with marzipan alone.

The cakes featured here use very simple skills to create very effective designs. The Simnel Cake is the classic Easter cake with its characteristic eleven balls representing the eleven loyal apostles. The Basket Cake is much simpler than it looks and requires no special equipment, all the flowers are made from simple discs and balls of marzipan which en masse look really effective.

TYPES OF MARZIPAN

Marzipan is basically a paste made from a mixture of nibbed almonds and sugar. The proportion of almonds to sugar varies according to the manufacturer, and some commercial marzipans include ground apricot or peach kernels or, occasionally, ground soya beans or soyflour. Egg white or whole egg is sometimes added for special purposes. The three most common types of marzipan available are white marzipan, yellow marzipan and raw sugar marzipan.

White marzipan:　This is the marzipan used most by cake decorators, and it is usually made from nibbed almonds and sugar only. White marzipan can be used in all sugarcraft calling for marzipan. It takes colour well. As the various brands available in each country may differ slightly, choose a brand which is easy to work with, neither too dry nor too sticky.
Yellow marzipan or almond icing: Yellow marzipan which is often used to cover rich fruit cake before icing, has permitted edible colouring added to a basic marzipan recipe. Because of the yellow dye, it does not colour well, and is therefore not recommended for sugarcraft work.
Raw sugar marzipan:　Available from health food shops and large supermarkets, this brown marzipan is made from nibbed almonds and unrefined sugar. It is sticky and does not model as well as white marzipan, and it does not take colour well. However, it has a pleasant flavour and can be used to cover cakes or for some marzipan sweets.

BUYING MARZIPAN

Marzipan can be purchased from cake decorating suppliers and from many supermarkets and health food stores. Always buy from a shop which has a rapid turnover, as stale marzipan will be hard and difficult to work with.

Most shops sell marzipan in foil or plastic wrapped packages in weights of either 250 g, 500 g, 1 kg or ½ lb, 1 lb, 2 lb. Some cake decorating suppliers make up their own packs in varying weights or will sell marzipan by the kilo or pound.

HOMEMADE MARZIPAN

Most cake decorators use commercial marzipan because homemade marzipan is often sticky and more difficult to work with. However, this boiled almond paste has a good flavour and can be used for most sugarcraft work.

200 g (7 oz/1 ¾ Cups) caster (superfine) sugar
125 ml (4 fl oz/½ Cup) water
Pinch cream of tartar
155 g (5 oz/1 ¼ Cups) ground almonds
1 – 2 drops almond essence or extract
1 large egg white
Icing (confectioner's) sugar, for dusting
Makes about 375 g (12 oz)

Put sugar and water in a small saucepan and cook over low heat, stirring occasionally, until sugar is dissolved.

Add cream of tartar and quickly bring to the boil. Boil until it reaches a temperature of 116°C (240°F), or soft ball stage.

Remove from the heat and beat until mixture turns cloudy. Add ground almonds and almond essence or extract. Whisk egg white lightly and add to the pan. Return the pan to low heat and cook for 2 minutes, stirring constantly.

Lightly dust a board or worksurface with icing (confectioner's) sugar and turn out the paste. Cover with plastic film and leave until cold.

Knead the paste for 2 – 3 minutes, or until it is completely smooth and free of cracks. Wrap in a plastic bag and store in a cool, dry place.

MARZIPAN CHART

Cake size	13 cm (5 in) square 15 cm (6 in) round	15 cm (6 in) square 18 cm (7 in) round	18 cm (7 in) square 20 cm (8 in) square	20 cm (8 in) square 23 cm (9 in) round	23 cm (9 in) square 25 cm (10 in) round	25 cm (10 in) square 28 cm (11 in) round	28 cm (11 in) square 30 cm (12 in) round
Apricot glaze	15 ml (3 teaspoons)	22.5 ml (4 ½ teaspoons)	30 ml (6 teaspoons)	37.5 ml (8 teaspoons)	45 ml (9 teaspoons)	45 ml (9 teaspoons)	60 ml (2 fl oz/ ¼ Cup)
Marzipan	375 g (12 oz)	750 g (1 ½ lb)	875 g (1 ¾ lb)	1 kg (2 lb)	1.25 kg (2 ½ lb)	1.5 kg (3 lb)	1.75 kg (3 ½ lb)

UNCOOKED MARZIPAN

This uncooked marzipan is good for modelling.

250 g (8 oz/2 Cups) ground almonds
450 g (1 lb/4 Cups) sifted icing (confectioner's) sugar
2 egg whites, lightly beaten.

Sift icing (confectioner's) sugar into a bowl with ground almonds.

Make a well in centre and add lightly beaten egg whites.

Stir together to form a firm paste. Knead until smooth.

WORKING WITH MARZIPAN

Marzipan is an easy medium to work with, and the same basic rules apply to all marzipan work. As in all sugarcraft, hygiene is important. Be sure that all worksurfaces are clean and free from any dust or grease. Some of the new plastic nonstick boards and rolling pins make the work much easier. All equipment should be thoroughly cleaned as well. Always wash hands and clean fingernails before beginning work. Some cake decorators wear thin plastic surgical gloves to ensure cleanliness.

Colouring marzipan: Edible food colours are available in liquid and paste form, but paste colours are best for marzipan. Liquid colours may change the consistency of the marzipan.

To colour marzipan, cut off the amount necessary, place a small amount of paste colour in the centre, and knead until the colour is evenly distributed. To keep worksurfaces and hands clean, the marzipan can be placed in a plastic bag and kneaded. Always start with a small amount of colour. If the marzipan is too pale, add a little more colour and knead again. If it is too dark, knead in another small piece of marzipan. If making several identical figures or colouring marzipan to cover a cake, try to colour enough at one time, as it is sometimes difficult to match colours.

Painting on marzipan: Painted colours can be used to add eyelashes and other features to modelled figures. The marzipan must skin before painting, or the colours will sink in or run.

Never paint directly from the bottle of colour onto the marzipan. If using liquid colours, place some of the colours on greaseproof (waxed) paper first. Dip the brush into the colour, wipe on the paper until there are no streaks, then paint on the marzipan. If using paste colours, put a few drops of water on the paper, then add a small amount of paste colour and continue as before. If painting in several colours, be sure the first colour is dry before painting in the next one.

Rolling and cutting: When rolling out marzipan to make flat or cutout decorations, it is best to use one of the special plastic nonstick boards which are available. If working on a wooden or marble surface, dust it with a little icing (confectioner's) sugar to prevent the marzipan from sticking. Do not dust with flour or cornflour (cornstarch), as these can cause fermentation. Use a small nonstick rolling pin, or a wooden rolling pin or a piece of dowelling lightly dusted with icing (confectioner's) sugar.

Marzipan can be cut with a sharp knife, scissors, or flower, biscuit (cookie), or aspic cutters. Take care not to mark the worksurface. To remove cutouts from the board, carefully slip a small palette knife under the shape and lift it off slowly.

APRICOT GLAZE

500 g (1 lb/1½ Cups) apricot jam (jelly)
45 ml (3 tablespoons) water

Place jam (jelly) and water in a saucepan. Heat gently until jam has melted. Boil rapidly for 30 seconds, then strain through sieve. Rub through as much fruit as possible and discard the skins, as these cause the glaze to ferment.

Pour glaze back into the clean hot jar, which has been heated in the oven, and seal with the lid. Use as required.

Makes 500 g (1 lb/1½ Cups) glaze.

Marzipanning a Cake

A well marzipanned cake is essential if the top icing is to be smooth, even and blemish-free. The method of application is the same for all varieties of marzipan.

Unwrap the cake and remove the lining paper. Place the cake on the cake board and roll the top with a rolling pin to flatten slightly.

Brush the top of the cake with apricot glaze. Sprinkle the worksurface with sieved icing (confectioner's) sugar.

Using two-thirds of the marzipan, knead it until smooth. Roll out to a 5 mm (¼ inch) thickness to match the shape of the top of the cake.

Make sure the marzipan moves freely on the work surface inverting the cake on the centre of the marzipan shape.

Trim off the excess marzipan to within 1 cm (½ in) of the cake, then using a small flexible palette knife, press the marzipan until it is level with the side of the cake.

Turn the cake the right-side-up and place in the centre of the cake board. Brush the sides of the cake with warm apricot glaze.

Knead the trimmings together, taking care not to include any crumbs from the cake. Measure and cut a piece of string the length of one side of a square cake or the circumference of a round cake. Measure and cut another piece of string the depth of the side of the cake from the board to the top.

Roll out the marzipan to 5 mm (¼ in) thickness and cut one side piece for a round cake and four pieces for a square cake, to match the length and width of the string. Knead the trimmings together and re-roll if necessary.

Carefully fit the marzipan on the side of the cake and smooth the joins with a palette knife. Leave in a warm, dry place for at least 24 hours to dry before icing.

1   *Roll the top of the fruit cake to flatten the fruit.*

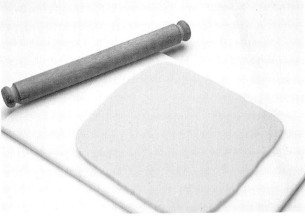

2   *Brush the top with warm apricot glaze.*

3   *Roll out the marzipan on a lightly sugared surface.*

4   *Marzipan rolled out to 5 mm (¼ in) thickness.*

5 *Fruit cake inverted onto centre of marzipan. Trim the marzipan to within 1 cm (½ in) of the cake.*

6 *Use a small palette knife and press the excess marzipan into the side, making it level with the edge of the cake.*

7 *Inverted cake on the cake board, with a flat square top.*

8 *Use two pieces of string to measure the width and length of the side of the cake and cut the marzipan strip to size.*

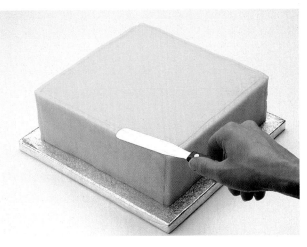

9 *Fit the marzipan strip onto the side of apricot-glazed cake.*

10 *Use a small palette knife to smooth all the joins together.*

MARZIPANNING A CAKE FOR SUGARPASTE

Measure the cake with a piece of string; up one side, across the top and down the other side. The marzipan should be rolled out a little larger than this measurement.

Turn the cake upside down to provide a good flat surface and stick on a board with a little softened marzipan. If the edges of the cake do not sit level on the cake board, make a sausage of marzipan and push into the gaps with a palette knife. Fill any visible holes and repair damaged corners with marzipan. Smooth over the cake.

To apply, lift up the left side of the marzipan and lay it over your right arm. Lift your arm and drape the bottom of the marzipan against the side of the cake; the right side of the marzipan should still lie on the board. Drape over the top of the cake, transfer marzipan to the left hand and support it while you remove air bubbles by brushing your right hand across the top of the cake.

Skirt out the corners and, using the flat of your hand, smooth the marzipan to the side of the cake with an upward movement. If a downward movement is used, it drags the marzipan and weakens the paste at the corners and edges. Use smoothers to eliminate any finger marks and bumps. Smooth the corners and upper edge using your warm hands. Place the flat edge of a palette knife against the cake at the base and cut away excess.

Smooth marzipan over cake sides.

Trim away excess marzipan.

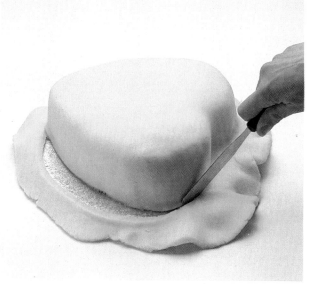

Cake ready for sugarpaste finish.

46

SIMPLE DECORATIONS

Marzipan is smooth, soft, easy to work and an ideal base for royal icing and sugarpaste. It can be coloured in various shades with food colourings, cut into shapes and moulded into flowers, animals and figures.

Used as a cake covering on its own, it combines colour, texture and flavour without the sweetness of icing (confectioner's) sugar. Once the cake has been covered in marzipan it can be decorated very simply by crimping the edges, applying cutouts, inlays and marzipan marquetry.

FRILLING MARZIPAN
Roll out thin strips of marzipan, making sure the strips move freely. Roll a cocktail stick (toothpick) or the end of a fine paintbrush backwards and forwards creating a thin frilled edge. Make several pieces and apply around the base or sides of the cake, securing with apricot glaze.

CUTOUTS
This is a simple way of decorating a cake with coloured marzipan cut into a variety of shapes. Tint several pieces of marzipan with food colourings to the required colours. Roll out evenly on a sugared surface until about 3 mm ($\frac{1}{8}$ in) thick. Using small aspic, cocktail or biscuit (cookie) cutters, cut out a variety of shapes. Arrange the cutout shapes in an attractive design on the cake and secure with apricot glaze.

Small flower and leaf cutters may be used to make a flower design; an arrangement of stems and other leaves can be cut out from thin strips of coloured marzipan.

47

CHRISTMAS CANDLES

Roll out bright red marzipan and use a ruler and a sharp knife to cut three different-sized candles. Place on a board or on top of an iced cake. To make the flames cut a yellow marzipan circle using a round cutter, then cut the flame shape from the edge of the circle. Mark the centre with a thin red sausage and position over the candles. Pipe white icing for drippings. Arrange holly leaves around the candles, if wished.

CRIMPER DESIGNS

These quick, easy and effective designs are created with crimping tools which are available from most kitchen shops or cake decorating suppliers. They come in different shapes: straight, curve, scallops, ovals, 'V', hearts, diamonds and zig-zag. To obtain an even crimped design, it is helpful to place an elastic band over the crimpers to prevent them springing apart and to adjust the size of the opening to give the required pattern. Try out the design on a spare piece of marzipan before decorating the cake.

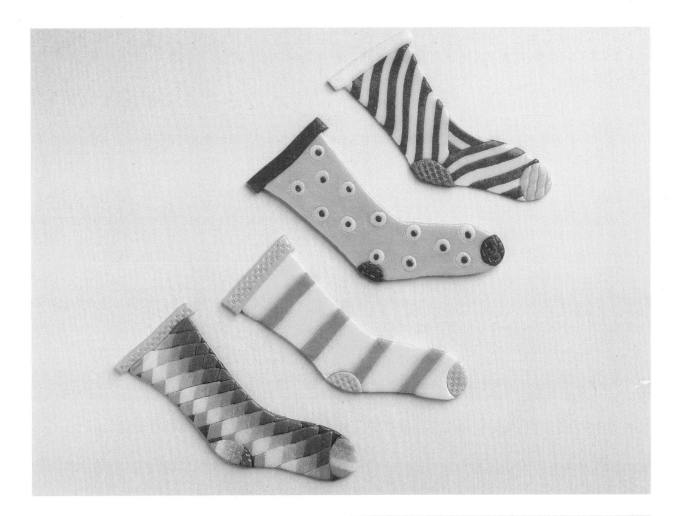

MARQUETRY

Colourful marzipan marquetry can be used to make flat cutout decorations, such as clothing for marzipan models. Colour the same amount of paste for each stripe, put them side by side and roll out thinly using spacers. Cut diagonally in strips and move each strip up one colour at a time to make the pattern. Re-roll to join into a sheet.

To make the flat Christmas stockings, use marquetry and inlay marzipan. Trace the photograph to make a cardboard template. Make sections of marquetry and inlay as above, then cut round the template using a sharp knife. Cut contrasting coloured strips for the tops and small round sections for the toes and heels. Mark with a nutmeg grater to get the effect of darning.

SNOWMAN

A jolly snowman makes a charming flat decoration to top a plain Christmas cake or winter birthday cake. Use the photograph to make a template, then cut out the snowman from white marzipan which has been rolled thinly. Mark features with a half-moon tool or a small ball tool, and position an orange oval nose. Make the hat from dark brown marzipan using the photograph as a guide. Make pipe, bow-tie and buttons from brightly coloured marzipan.

49

SIMNEL CAKE

This Easter cake has a layer of marzipan baked into the centre of it. Sometimes the marzipan on top is lightly toasted before adding decoration. Simply place the cake under a medium grill (broiler) for 1 – 2 minutes until the top is lightly browned. The eleven balls of marzipan on top represent each of the apostles, with the exception of Judas, of course.

250 g (8 oz/2 Cups) self raising flour
5 ml (1 teaspoon) mixed spice
185 g (6 oz/¾ Cup) butter
185 g (6 oz/¾ Cup) dark brown sugar
3 eggs
15 ml (3 teaspoons milk)
500 g (1 lb/3 Cups) mixed fruit
60 g (2 oz/⅓ Cup) glacé (candied) cherries, rinsed and
chopped
625 g (1¼ lb) white marzipan
3 tablespoons sieved apricot glaze
Orange paste food colouring
1 metre (1 yd) 2.5 cm (1 in) silk ribbon

Grease and line an 18 cm (7 in) round cake tin (pan). Preheat oven to 160C (325F/Gas 3).

Sift flour and spice together. Cream butter and brown sugar together until light and fluffy. Gradually beat in eggs, adding a little flour with each addition to prevent it from curdling. Mix in fruit and cherries with flour and milk until a soft dropping consistency.

Add half of mixture to tin. Roll 125 g (4 oz) marzipan to an 18 cm (7 in) circle to fit the cake tin. Lay on the cake mixture in the tin, then cover with the remaining cake mixture. Level the top and bake in the centre of the oven for 2 hours, or until a skewer inserted into the centre comes out clean; leave to cool in tin.

Brush top of the cake with 2 tablespoons apricot glaze. Roll out 315 g (10 oz) marzipan to an 18 cm (7 in) circle to fit the top. Press onto cake, then mark a diamond pattern across top with ruler or blunt-bladed knife. Pin edges together between finger and thumb and flute up edges.

Roll 60 g (2 oz) marzipan into 11 balls and arrange these round the edge of the marzipan circle attaching each with a dab of jam.

Take the remaining 125 g (4 oz) marzipan and colour half with orange paste food colouring. Roll both halves into long sausage shapes, then twist loosely together. Place round base of the cake then join together neatly. With any remaining pieces make a small circle to fit into the centre of cake. Finish off with a ribbon.

BASKET OF FLOWERS

20 cm (8 in) square sponge or light fruit cake
1 kg (2 lb) white marzipan
Brown, yellow, orange, pink and gooseberry green paste food
colourings
5 tablespoons sieved apricot glaze
Icing (confectioner's) sugar

Place the cake on a board. Roll out 60 g (2 oz) marzipan very thinly to a 20 cm (8 in) square and place on top of the cake, which has been brushed with 1 tablespoon apricot glaze. Brush the sides of the cake with 4 tablespoons apricot glaze.

To make the basket weave: Colour 375 g (12 oz) marzipan light brown and leave 375 g (12 oz) plain then cut each piece into four equal portions. Roll each piece into a strip 25 x 7.5 cm (10 x 2½ in). Cut the white strip into five long strips 1.5 cm (½ in) wide. Cut the brown strip into short strips 1.5 cm (½ in) wide. Place the five white strips on a surface dusted with icing (confectioner's) sugar and thread one brown strip between them. Take the next brown strip and weave it in the opposite way. Complete the woven strip by using up all of the pieces. Prop the cake up by placing a small box under the board. The cake should be tilting up towards you. Carefully lift the woven strip onto the cake with both hands, place centrally on the side to be covered, press on firmly, then trim both ends with kitchen scissors. Mould the top edge over the cake and towards the centre. Do not worry if this is jagged as it will be covered with flowers. Continue to cover the other three sides.

To make the simple flowers: Divide the remaining marzipan into five, leave one piece plain and colour the rest green, yellow, orange and pink.

Orange flowers: Roll out the orange marzipan thinly then stamp out into 15 x 3.5 cm (1½ in) rounds using a plain pastry cutter. Flute the edges of the flower by rolling with a cocktail stick (toothpick). Make a centre from a ball of plain marzipan, insert into the middle, then pinch together. Make 15 flowers and leave to dry out for 2 hours.

Pink flowers: Roll out the pink marzipan thinly, and stamp out 15 plain rounds using a 3.5 cm (1½ in) plain cutter. Snip petals by making small cuts all round with kitchen scissors, make centres from small round balls of plain marzipan. Insert into the centre of each flower then pinch together and flute out the petals. Make a star pattern in the centre of each flower with the tip of a star icing tube.

Daisies: Roll out the plain marzipan thinly and stamp out 35 small daisy shapes with a small fluted cutter. Make into a rounded shape over your knuckle. Make a yellow ball-shaped centre for each flower, then press into the centre. Mark holes with a skewer and leave to dry out for 2 hours.

Leaves: Roll out the green marzipan thinly and cut out 30 leaf shapes with a leaf cutter or the point of a small sharp knife. Mark veins onto the leaves with the base of the knife, then leave to dry out for 2 hours.

Pink bell flowers: Roll remaining pink scraps into small balls. Mould each ball down over the top of a moulding tool or ballpoint pen cover. Pull into a bell shape, then make a centre from plain scraps, insert in the middle and pinch together.

To assemble: Dampen the flowers with water and place them on top of the cake interspersed with the leaves. You will have enough flowers to cover the top completely.

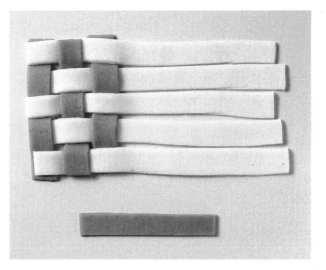

Weaving the marzipan.

Making orange flowers (above).
Making pink flowers, daisies,
leaves and pink bell flowers (below).

QUICK ICINGS AND FROSTINGS

Basic buttercream icing can be used to great effect whether to create a novelty-type cake, a sponge-type birthday cake or an elegant gâteau. For a more sophisticated finish there is the classic crème au buerre which takes longer to prepare but has a lovely glossy texture. There is the recipe for a rich, dark chocolate fudge icing which chocolate lovers are certain to enjoy or you could use the fluffy white American-style frosting which works particularly well with chocolate cakes.

The elegant gâteaux illustrated here have all been made with these toppings and decorated with fruit and nuts.

BUTTERCREAM

A versatile filling, icing or frosting for almost any type of cake, which can be spread evenly and patterned with a knife or scraper, or piped into designs using different icing tubes. Flavour with chocolate, coffee, orange or lemon rinds.

125 g (4 oz/½ Cup) butter, softened
250 g (8 oz/1 ¾ Cups) icing (confectioner's) sugar, sieved
10 ml (2 teaspoons) lemon juice
Few drops vanilla essence (extract)

VARIATIONS

15 ml (1 tablespoon) cocoa powder blended with 15 ml (3 teaspoons) boiling water
10 ml (2 teaspoons) instant coffee powder blended with 5 ml (1 teaspoon) of boiling water
10 ml (2 teaspoons) lemon, orange or lime rind

1   *Beat the butter with a wooden spoon until light and fluffy.*

2   *Sift some of the sugar into the bowl. Stir the sugar into the butter, then beat well after each addition.*

3   *Add the lemon juice or other flavourings and beat until smooth.*

QUICK ICING AND FROSTING QUANTITIES FOR BUTTERCREAM, CRÈME AU BUERRE AND AMERICAN ICING

Cake size	18 cm (7 in) square 18 – 20 cm (7 – 8 in) round	20 cm (8 in) square 23 cm (9 in) round	23 cm (9 – 10 in) square 25 – 27.5 cm (10 – 11 in) round
Icing and Frosting Quantity	250 g (8 oz/1 ¾ Cups)	375 g (12 oz/2⅔ Cups)	500 g (1 lb/3 ½ Cups)

4 Use a cocktail stick to add food colouring to the buttercream. Beat the food colouring into the buttercream.

5 Spread the buttercream onto the top of the cake using a small palette knife.

6 Smooth the buttercream using a small palette knife dipped into hot water.

CRÈME AU BEURRE

A light-textured buttercream suitable for large and small cakes, which keeps the cakes moist. It spreads or pipes well, giving a glossy finish. For best results, make and use it when required; do not chill or freeze until it has been applied to the cake.

90 g (3 oz/6 tablespoons) caster (superfine) sugar
60 ml (4 tablespoons) water
2 egg yolks, beaten
155 g (5 oz/generous ½ Cup) unsalted (sweet) butter,
  softened
Makes 250 g (8 oz/1 ¾ Cup)

1   *Measure the water and sugar into a saucepan. Dissolve sugar in the water to form sugar solution before boiling to a syrup.*

2   *Boil rapidly for 1 minute until the syrup reaches thread stage (107°C/225°F). Test by placing a little syrup between two teaspoons: when pulled apart, a thread of syrup forms.*

3   *Pour a thin stream of sugar syrup into the beaten egg yolks.*

4   *Whisk well after each addition. Whisk the mixture until light and thick. Allow to cool.*

VARIATIONS

Chocolate Crème au beurre: add 60 g (2 oz/2 squares) melted plain (semisweet) chocolate.

Lemon or orange crème au beurre: add 1 teaspoon grated lemon or orange rind.

Liqueur-flavoured crème au beurre: add 3–4 teaspoons of contreau, apricot brandy or other liqueur.

5 *Beat the butter with a wooden spoon until light and fluffy.*

6 *Pour the egg mixture into the butter.*

7 *Whisk the mixture gently after each addition until light and creamy.*

8 *Add any flavourings at this stage, if required, and use a spatula to mix carefully without beating. Use at once.*

AMERICAN FROSTING

A pure white icing (frosting) that is light in texture and can be flavoured or coloured if desired. As the icing is white, tinting with food colouring is more accurate.

500 g (1 lb/2 Cups) granulated sugar
150 ml (5 fl oz/½ Cup) water
Pinch of cream of tartar
2 egg whites

Put sugar and water into a small pan, add cream of tartar and stir over a gentle heat. Do not allow to boil. When sugar has dissolved bring to the boil and boil rapidly until the temperature reaches 120°C (240°F) on a sugar thermometer. Beat egg white until stiff and pour boiling sugar syrup into it, beating hard. Continue to beat until mixture begins to thicken and dull slightly. Quickly turn out onto cake and spread with a palette knife.

VARIATIONS
15 ml (3 teaspoons) cocoa powder blended with 15 ml (3 teaspoons) boiling water
10 ml (2 teaspoons) instant coffee powder blended with 5 ml (1 teaspoon) of boiling water
10 ml (2 teaspoons) lemon, orange or lime rind.

QUICK FROSTING

A quickly-made icing (frosting) suitable for pouring over the cakes to give a smooth, satin finish or for spreading with a knife to give a textured appearance.

60 g (2 oz/¼ Cup) butter
45 ml (3 tablespoons) milk
250 g (8 oz/1½ Cups) icing (confectioner's) sugar, sieved

Half-fill a saucepan with water and bring to the boil, then remove from heat. Place butter, milk and icing sugar in a heatproof bowl over a saucepan of hot water. Stir this occasionally until melted, then beat with a wooden spoon until smooth.

Use immediately to pour over a cake to coat evenly, or leave until thicker, then spread over a cake to give a textured finish.

This quantity will cover an 18–20 cm (7–8 in) square cake, or a 20–23 cm (8–9 in) round cake.

VARIATIONS
Fruit or Coffee Frosting: replace milk with any flavour fruit juice, or strong black coffee.
Fudge Frosting: replace 90 g (3 oz/¾ Cup) of icing (confectioner's) sugar with dark, soft brown sugar.

Chocolate Frosting: add 15 ml (3 teaspoons) of cocoa powder to the icing (confectioner's) sugar or 60 g (2 oz/2 squares) of plain (semi-sweet or unsweetened) chocolate to the milk and butter.

GLACÉ ICING

Suitable for quickly decorating small cakes, Swiss (jelly) jam rolls or tops of cakes.

250 g (8 oz/1½ Cups) icing (confectioner's) sugar, sieved
30–45 ml (2–3 tablespoons) boiling water

Place sugar in a bowl; using a wooden spoon, gradually stir in water until icing is the same consistency as thick cream. Tint with food colouring if desired.

VARIATIONS
Add 10 ml (2 teaspoons) cocoa to the sugar.
Replace the water with any fruit juice, or strong black coffee.

CREAM CHEESE ICING

This icing (frosting) is often found on cheesecakes but is equally good on chocolate cakes.

90 g (3 oz) cream cheese
60 g (2 oz/½ Cup) butter
600 g (1¼ lb/4 Cups) icing (confectioner's) sugar, approx. 1 teaspoon vanilla essence (extract)
2 teaspoons grated lemon rind

Beat cream cheese and butter together until light and fluffy. Fold in icing (confectioner's) sugar until thick enough to spread, stir in vanilla and lemon rind.

This quantity will fill and ice two 20 cm (8 in) round cakes.

MARSHMALLOW ICING

A rich icing (frosting) that looks attractive swirled or rough iced and decorated with purchased decorations. It is particularly good with chocolate cake and is excellent as a quick icing (frosting) for a children's cake.

2 egg whites
185 g (6 oz/1½ Cups) caster (superfine) sugar
¼ teaspoon cream of tartar
3 teaspoons golden syrup (light corn syrup)
90 ml (3 fl oz/⅓ Cup) water
12 large white marshmallows cut into quarters

In a bowl over a pan of boiling water combine egg whites, sugar, cream of tartar, syrup and water. Beat with an electric mixer on a low speed for about 1 minute, then increase speed of mixer to high and continue to beat for 7 minutes or until icing (frosting) is thick and creamy. Remove from heat and stir in marshmallows. Continue beating until marshmallows have melted.

This quantity will fill and ice a three layer 23 cm (9 in) cake.

CHOCOLATE FUDGE ICING

A rich chocolate icing (frosting) suitable for coating, filling and piping onto cakes. Use the icing immediately to give a smooth, glossy finish or leave it to thicken, then spread with a small palette knife to give a swirly textured finish.

125 g (4 oz/4 squares) plain (semi-sweet or unsweetened) chocolate
60 g (2 oz/¼ Cup) butter
1 egg, beaten
185 g (6 oz/1 Cup) icing (confectioner's) sugar, sieved

Half-fill a saucepan with water and bring to the boil, then remove from the heat. Place the chocolate and butter in a heatproof bowl over the saucepan of hot water. Stir this occasionally until melted.

Add the egg and stir with a wooden spoon until mixed together and well blended. Remove the bowl from the saucepan, stir in the sugar and beat until smooth.

Use immediately for pouring over a cake smoothly or leave to cool for a thicker consistency.

This quantity will cover an 18–20 cm (7–8 in) square cake, or a 20–23 cm (8–9 in) round cake.

SIMPLE DECORATIONS

Buttercream is easy to use for decorating a cake. It can be coloured and flavoured, used as a cake covering, topping, filling and for piping. The consistency remains the same for all finishes.

ICED TOP AND COATED SIDES
Sandwich a sponge cake together with buttercream and spread the sides to coat evenly. Press chopped nuts, coconut, chocolate strands (vermicelli) or crushed macaroons on to the side of the cake to coat evenly. Spread the top as evenly and smoothly as possible. Make a pretty edging with red and green coloured cherries cut into thin slices and arranged around the edge, or arranged with a selection of marzipan fruits or sugar flowers.

SCRAPER DESIGN
A side scraper can produce a very attractive pattern when used to smooth the icing on the sides and top of a cake, or in a zig-zag movement on the top. It looks like a plastic side scraper but the edge is serrated rather than flat.

Spread the top and sides of the cake with Crème au Beurre, buttercream, chocolate or American icing (frosting). Place the side scraper onto the side of the cake and pull across or around the side in one movement to make the pattern. Repeat to pattern the top if desired and decorate with fruit rinds cut into tiny shapes using aspic cutters, chocolate dots, nuts, cherries, angelica or sugar flowers.

FINISHES WITH SIMPLE ICINGS
Lines: Buttercream lends itself to various finishes, being soft and easy to spread. Try using a small palette knife to create an attractive finish. Spread

the top and sides of a cake with buttercream, crème au beurre, chocolate or American icing (frosting). Using a small palette knife on the top of the cake, spread the icing backwards and forwards in a continuous movement to make a lined pattern. To create the same pattern on the sides, place the palette knife at the base of the cake and work up and down, pressing the knife into the icing marking the same pattern. Use a few nuts or sugar flowers to make a pretty border.

Peaks: These can also be formed in soft icing (frosting) just like royal icing peaks. Once the top and sides of a cake have been spread evenly with icing, press a small palette knife onto the icing and pull sharply away to form a peak. Ensure the icing is not too firm or the palette knife may pull the sponge cake away with it, causing crumbs. Peak the side, working around the top of the cake and gradually down to the base, keeping the top smooth. Arrange some mimosa balls and angelica, or split almonds and crystallized violets to make a flower design.

Edible Decorations: Many ingredients can make attractive decorations. Place some cocoa or coffee on a piece of absorbent paper, then dip a skewer into the powder and press onto an iced cake to make a line. Repeat, marking lines in both directions to form a lattice design. Very fine lines of chopped nuts may be used in the same way. Melted chocolate drizzled on to the surface makes a cake look special.

Coloured Swirls: The use of coloured icing spread into swirls over the surface is a simple way of introducing colours onto a cake iced (frosted) with buttercream. Spread the top and sides of a cake with buttercream; smooth with a palette knife. Tint a small quantity of buttercream. Use a small palette knife, dip into the tinted icing, evenly spaced, over the top and sides of the cake. Try several shades of one colour or contrasting colours to give a variety of swirls on the cake.

DECORATING IDEA

MAYPOLE CAKE

Fill basic sponge cake with jam (jelly). Cover the cake and board with green-coloured buttercream. Use a teaspoon to press green-coloured coconut onto cake sides and board. Draw fork across top of cake to make swirls, decorate edges with row of piped stars, if desired. Arrange sugar flowers into buttercream while still soft.

Push drinking straw into centre of cake and place circle of flowers around base. Cut synthetic ribbon into 30 cm (12 in) lengths and curl each length by pulling across a blunt knife. Secure ribbons to straw top with sticky tape, anchor the other ends to the cake with buttercream and flowers. Tie a bow round top of straw to hide tape. Decorate with flowers.

CITRUS GRAPE GÂTEAU

20 cm (8 in) square lemon-flavoured sponge cake
Lemon or lime curd
155 ml (5 fl oz/½ Cup) double (heavy) cream, whipped
Buttercream made with 125 g (4 oz/½ Cup) butter, 250 g
 (8 oz/1½ Cups) icing (confectioner's) sugar
125 g (4 oz/1 Cup) chopped toasted hazelnuts
Glacé icing made with 315 g (10 oz/2 Cups) icing
 (confectioner's) sugar
Green, yellow food colouring
Piping gel (optional)
Frosted grapes
Small pieces of fern

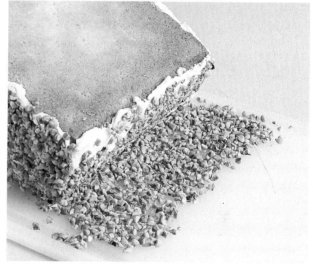

Cut sponge in half and spread with lemon curd and then double (heavy) cream. Position other half on top. Spread a little buttercream around the sides of the cake and coat with chopped nuts. Place on a board or plate. Make up the glacé icing. Colour a small quantity green and a small quantity yellow. Spread the white icing over the top of the cake and then pipe green and yellow lines across the top. Immediately draw a skewer through the lines to feather the icing (piping gel may be coloured and used for piping the lines to give a more glossy effect). Using a piping bag fitted with a star tube, pipe the remaining buttercream around the top edge of the cake (see page 97 for further details). Decorate with frosted grapes or plain grapes if preferred, and fern.

VARIATION

For a simple effect, colour the buttercream yellow. Omit the glacé icing and gel. Spread a layer of buttercream over the top of the cake and pipe remainder around the top edge (illustrated on cover).

FROSTED LAZY DAISY CAKE

3-egg quantity orange flavoured basic sponge mix, cooked
   in a 23 cm (9 in) ring mould
American frosting (see page 58)
Peach food colouring
2 – 3 dried apricots
1 – 2 pieces stem ginger
Pecan nuts
Orange peel curls

American frosting sets quickly, so prepare the
decorations before icing the cake. Using a small
round cutter, cut the apricots and ginger into small
circles for daisy centres. Count out sufficient nuts
to make petals around each centre.

Using a canelle knife, cut thin strips of orange
rind, and curl into spirals. Place the ring cake on
a board or plate. Make frosting following
instructions. Add peach colouring. Spread over cake
making swirls while spreading. Quickly arrange the
nuts, apricots, ginger and orange curls on the cake
to resemble lazy daisies.

CHOCOLATE AND PISTACHIO GÂTEAU

4-egg quantity chocolate sponge mix baked in a 33 x 11 x
   6 cm (13 x 4 x 2 in) loaf tin (pan)
Chocolate fudge icing
Chocolate crème au beurre
10 small choux buns (see opposite)
1 quantity caramel (see opposite)
Pistachio nuts in shells

Place the cake on a plate or board. Cover with
chocolate fudge icing. Put a little creme au berre into
a piping bag with a small tube and fill the choux
buns. Pipe the remaining crème au beurre around
the base of the cake. Reserve 8 – 12 pistachios in their
shells. Chop the remaining nuts, if necessary, add
a little green colouring to brighten the colour. Make
the caramel. Using tongs, quickly dip each choux
bun in caramel and then place on top of cake.
Sprinkle with nuts. Any remaining caramel can be
trickled over the cake and more nuts scattered on
top. Arrange the pistachios in their shells at each
corner of the base of the cake.

CHOUX PASTRY

30 g (1 oz/6 teaspoons) butter
75 ml (2½ fl oz/⅓ Cup) water
30 g (1 oz/¼ Cup) plain (all purpose) flour
1 small egg, beaten

Melt butter in water in a saucepan and bring to the boil. Remove from heat. Tip flour at once into pan. Beat well until mixture leaves sides of pan clean. Gradually beat in the until mixture is smooth and glossy. Put into a piping bag fitted with a plain 1 cm (½ in) tube. Pipe 10–12 small balls on a baking sheet. Bake at 220C (425F/Gas 7) for 15–20 minutes. Make slits in bottom of balls to allow steam out. Cool.

CARAMEL

250 g (8 oz/1 Cup) sugar
125 ml (4 fl oz/½ Cup) water

Dissolve sugar in water over gentle heat, then cook until caramel in colour. Remove from heat and use immediately.

Adding green colouring to pistachio nuts.

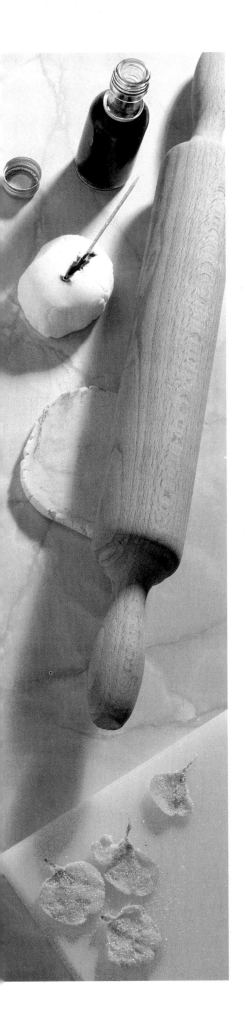

SUGARPASTE

The art of using sugarpaste is easy to master making it possible to create beautiful cakes relatively quickly. Sugarpaste may be laid over sponge-type cakes over a layer of jam (jelly) or buttercream and iced directly or it may be laid on top of a layer of dried marzipan. The cake can then be decorated with piped royal icing or special sugarpaste techniques may be applied including simple colour and cutout work.

The cakes show how effective sugarpaste can be. The Christmas cake is made from a variety of cutout letters and holly leaves while the streaky cake shows that very simple marbling can create an elegant finished cake. Later in the chapter there are examples of painted cakes which demonstrate how yet another basic skill can be applied to this versatile medium.

RECIPES

SUGARPASTE

15 g (½ oz) gelatine
60 ml (2 fl oz/¼ Cup) cold water
22 g (¾ oz) glycerine
125 ml (4 fl oz/½ Cup) liquid glucose
1 kg (2 lb/6 Cups) icing (confectioner's) sugar

Soak gelatine in cold water and place over hot water until dissolved and clear. (Do not allow gelatine to boil.)

Add glycerine and glucose to gelatine. Stir until melted. Add mixture to sieved sugar. Knead to a soft consistency.

MODELLING PASTE

This paste is malleable and easily stretched which makes it ideal for bas relief.

250 g (8 oz/1½ Cups) icing (confectioner's) sugar
15 ml (3 teaspoons) gum tragacanth
5 ml (1 teaspoon) liquid glucose
30 ml (6 teaspoons) cold water

Sieve sugar with gum tragacanth. Add liquid glucose and cold water to sugar and mix well. Knead to form a soft dough.

Combine with an equal weight of sugarpaste. Leave 24 hours before using.

If the paste is dry, work in a little white fat (shortening) or egg white as needed. If the paste is sticky, add cornflour (cornstarch) as needed.

Basic techniques applied to sugarpasted cakes.

BASIC TECHNIQUES

Most beginners can successfully cover a cake with sugarpaste but a professional finish – a glossy surface free of cracks and air bubbles with smooth rounded corners – will only result from practice. Try not to cover a cake under artificial light as flaws are not as clearly defined as in daylight. It is difficult to hide any imperfections on the covering as these may occur where you don't want to add decorations. Don't panic if the covering starts to go wrong; it can always be removed and reapplied.

There are many techniques that can be used to decorate the covered cake. Crimping, embossing and ribbon insertion are done when the paste is still soft. These simple techniques may help to hide the imperfections of a poor surface.

More advanced techniques are bas relief and appliqué, the addition of frills and flounces, embroidery and lace.

Store unused paste in a plastic bag or airtight container in a cool, dry place.

The sugarpaste on the cake will soon skin, or become firm on the surface. Store the cake in a dry place out of direct sunlight which may fade the colours. A cardboard box is the ideal container; a sealed plastic container causes the cake to sweat and the icing may not skin.

COMMERCIAL SUGARPASTE

Although there are many recipes for homemade sugarpaste, there are certainly times when ready-made pastes are better or more convenient to use.

There are several types of sugarpaste on the market, basically the same kind of recipe but packaged under different names. Textures may vary and some are easier to work with than others. It is a good idea to try a small quantity first to see if it is suitable for the job you require, before purchasing a large quantity.

Sugarpaste is available from large supermarkets and cake decorating shops from 250 g (8 oz) packs up to 5 kg (12 lb) boxes, it may be tinted any shade and used very successfully for covering cakes, and for modelling into sugar decorations.

SUGARPASTE QUANTITIES

Cake sizes	13 cm (5 in) square 15 cm (6 in) round	15 cm (6 in) square 18 cm (7 in) round	18 cm (7 in) square 20 cm (8 in) round	20 cm (8 in) square 23 cm (9 in) round	23 cm (9 in) square 25 cm (10 in) round	25 cm (10 in) square 28 cm (11 in) round	28 cm (11 in) square 30 cm (12 in) round
Sugar-paste	500 g (1 lb)	750 g (1 ½ lb)	875 g (1 ¾ lb)	1 kg (2 lb)	1.25 kg (2 ½ lb)	1.5 kg (3 lb)	1.75 kg (3 ½ lb)

COVERING A CAKE WITH SUGARPASTE

1 *Brush the cake with sherry or cooled, boiled water to moisten the surface of the marzipan so that the sugarpaste will stick.*

2 *Roll out the sugarpaste on a lightly icing (confectioner's)-sugared surface.*

3 *Support the sugarpaste with the rolling pin and unroll, over the top of the marzipanned cake.*

4 *The cake completely covered by the sugarpaste.*

5 *Gently press the sugarpaste onto the cake, starting at the top and carefully smoothing around the sides so that the excess sugarpaste is at the base of the cake on the board.*

6 *Use a knife to trim away the excess sugarpaste from the base of the cake.*

SUGARPASTED BOARD

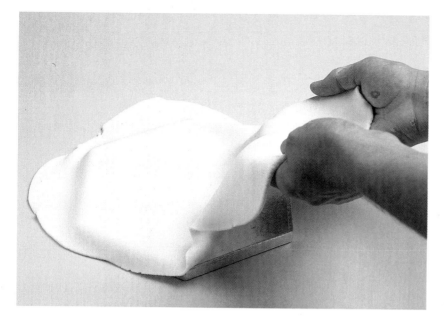

1 *Roll out the sugarpaste in the required colours 5 mm (¼ in) thick. Lift up and drape across the board.*

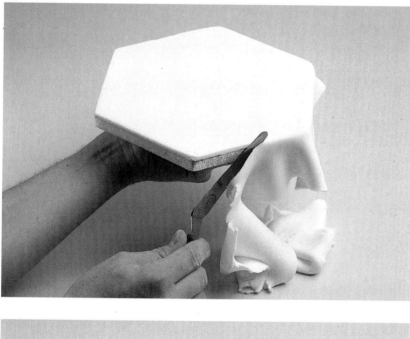

2 *Cut off the excess paste using a palette knife, taking care to keep the edge straight.*

3 *The finished board covered with sugarpaste is left to dry thoroughly before the sugarpasted cake is positioned.*

COLOURING SUGARPASTE

Adding colour to sugarpaste is better done in natural light, as artificial light can affect colour perception.

Add a little at a time; more can always be added later. If the colour is too dark, add another piece of paste and knead again. A pale base colour generally looks more pleasing and nicely sets off the colours of the flowers, ribbons, and other decorations.

To colour a large amount of paste, divide into small pieces, colour each one, then knead all the pieces together to blend.

After kneading in the colour, cut the paste in half to see if streaks are visible. If so, re-knead and cut again until all streaking has disappeared.

Streaks can however be used to create a marbled effect. To achieve this, colour is kneaded into the paste slightly. When the paste is rolled out, the surface has a definite streaky pattern.

PAINTING ON SUGARPASTE

Beginners often use conventional colour schemes. By experimentation and trial and error a good sense of colour should develop and more creative designs should be possible.

Avoid the temptation to use colour straight from the container as few of these basic colours are true to nature. Experiment with colour by mixing.

Harmonious colours are used to give a balanced appearance to a cake. Colours from opposite sides of the colour wheel can be used together to create a striking effect, as long as one of the colours is used for detail only.

It is possible to paint directly onto the surface of completely dry sugarpaste. Use paste or liquid food colour. If painting for the first time do not paint directly onto the cake's surface as it is difficult to remove mistakes. Instead paint onto a plaque which can be placed on a cake if wished.

When applying colour to sugarpaste, keep the brush fairly dry. Too much moisture will cause streaking and may affect the surface of the paste.

If painting a scene, subtle blending of colour can be achieved by brushing one colour into the next while both are still wet.

If a pattern or quilt with clear defined lines is to be painted, one colour should be completely dry before adjacent colour or surface pattern is applied.

If you plan to duplicate a favourite cake, make a note of how a certain colour has been achieved. This applies to painting onto paste as well as mixing colour into paste.

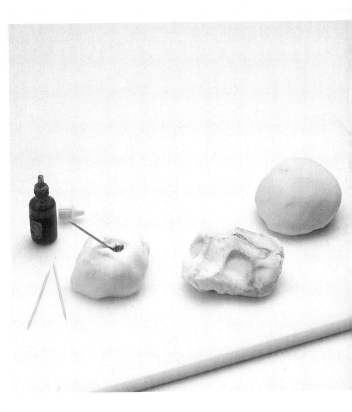

Colouring sugarpaste using paste colouring.

A cake with marbled sugarpaste.

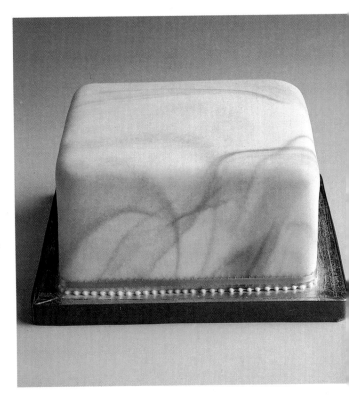

MAKING A PAINTED SUGARPASTE PLAQUE

1 *Use an oval or circular cutter to cut out the plaque from thinly rolled out sugarpaste.*

2 *Paint the design using fine paintbrushes and powdered food colourings with water.*

3 *The completed painted design.*

4 *A selection of painted sugar plaques.*

CRIMPING

Use the same method as marzipan crimping. Ensure the crimper is clean and dusted with cornflour (cornstarch). Only crimp on a freshly sugarpasted cake or the icing will be too rigid and may crack. Try out the design on a spare piece of sugarpaste before attempting to decorate the cake. Remember to release the crimper fully each time it is used to mark the pattern or the icing may tear.

CUTWORK

Cutwork is a technique in which biscuit (cookie), aspic and flower cutters are used to create simple sugarpaste shapes. More original and intricate designs can be achieved using cardboard templates.

If using templates make them out of fine card, such as the sides of cereal boxes, as this is durable and has a firm edge against which to place the scalpel when cutting. This will give a clean, sharp edge to the paste which is most important in cutwork. Use a sharp craft knife or scalpel. Nothing will spoil the overall effect more than indistinct shapes or damaged lines.

Place cutwork pieces on a piece of rolled sugarpaste, then give one firm roll to make patterned sheet of sugarpaste. Use as normal.

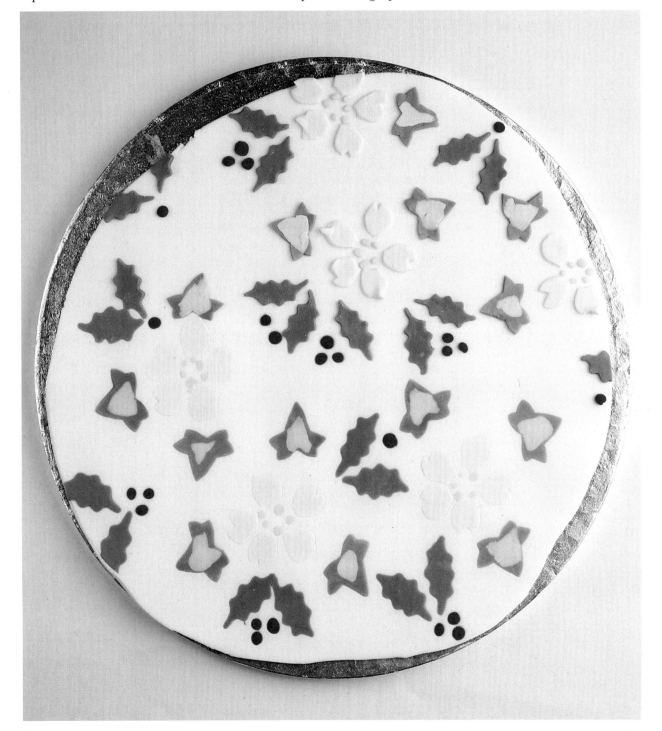

DECORATING IDEAS

GRADUATION CAKE

Cover the cake with marzipan and cream-coloured sugarpaste as usual extending the sugarpaste to cover part of the board, then within 30 minutes, use a No3 crimper to form a pattern around the edges. Place a thin ribbon around the base of the cake securing with dots of icing. Colour a little royal icing to a dark brown and pipe a decoration in the top left and bottom right corners of the cake, alternatively, use a brown food colouring pen. Make a scroll from rice paper and using the brown food-colouring pen, write the inscription on one side. Attach additional sheets of rice paper to the scroll and moisten to stick. Roll the ends of the paper scroll around two dowels and then moisten to attach the paper to itself and the dowels. Lightly moisten the bottom sheet of the scroll and attach to the cake.

BOOK CAKE

Make a line down the centre of the cake and carve out two sections to resemble the open pages of a book. Cover the cake in marzipan and sugarpaste as usual. With a long knife make a series of lines along the sides of the cake to represent the pages of the book. Pipe a shell around the base of the cake and leave to skin for 24 hours. Draw a design of your choice on a sheet of tracing paper and transfer the design to the cake. Paint on the design as instructed in this chapter. This is a good general purpose design that can be adapted to represent anyone's interests.

SUGAR FROSTED FLOWER CAKE

18 cm (7 in) square sponge or Madeira cake covered with
  sugarpaste
23 cm (9 in) square silver cake board
Small fresh yellow flowers
1 egg white, beaten
125 g (4 oz/1 Cup) caster (superfine) sugar
1 metre (1 yd) 5 mm (¼ in) yellow ribbon
1 metre (1 yd) 1 cm (½ in) fancy ribbon

Place sugarpasted cake in centre of cake board and
leave to dry.

To sugar frost flowers (see below): ensure they are
dry and fresh, trim stems to required length. Place
sugar in a shallow bowl. Using a fine paint brush,
paint each petal on both sides with egg white to coat
evenly; paint centre of stem. Carefully spoon sugar
over flower to coat evenly. Place flowers on a cooling
rack lined with absorbent paper and leave in a warm
place to dry completely and set hard.

Trim ribbons to fit around sides of cake, securing
with stainless steel pins. Tie eight tiny bows, and
pin in position. Arrange sugar frosted flowers on top
of cake.
Note: when using pins, take great care to remove
before eating. If presenting cake, give recipient a note
of how many pins were used to ensure that all are
safely removed.

MARBLED CELEBRATION CAKE

25 cm (10 in) hexagonal sponge or Madeira cake
30 ml (2 tablespoons) apricot glaze
30 cm (12 in) hexagonal cake board
1.25 kg (2½ lb) sugarpaste
Holly green food colouring
Icing (confectioner's) sugar, to dust
White and turquoise silk flowers
1 silver 'Congratulations' emblem

Lightly brush cake board and cake with apricot glaze.
Knead sugarpaste until smooth on a surface dusted
with icing (confectioner's) sugar. Press sugarpaste
into a flat round and drop several small drops of food
colouring over surface of sugarpaste (see below).
Knead the colouring into sugarpaste until streaked.

Roll out one-third and use to cover cake board,
trim surplus sugarpaste from edges using a knife.

Roll out remaining sugarpaste 7.5 cm (3 in) larger
than cake, support sugarpaste over a rolling pin and
unroll over the cake. Smooth over top of cake and
down sides, working surplus sugarpaste to the base.
Neaten the base of cake with a knife. Ensure the top
and sides of cake are smooth and glossy by polishing
the icing with the palm of the hand in circular
movements.

Place cake carefully on centre of cake board, leave
to dry. Using sugarpaste trimmings, shape neatly
into an oblong and press in silk flowers to make an
arrangement to sit on the board.

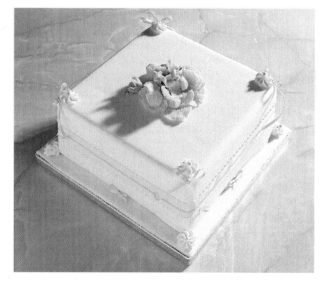

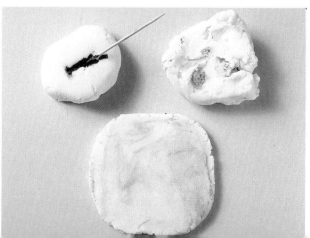

NOEL CHRISTMAS CAKE

*20 cm (8 in) round rich or light fruit cake, marzipanned
  and covered in sugarpaste*
25 cm (10 in) round silver cake board
Red and green food colourings
Cornflour (cornstarch)
1 metre (1 yd) 5 mm (¼ in) red and green ribbon

Place sugarpasted cake on centre of cake board, leave to dry.

Knead sugarpaste trimmings together until smooth, cut off two-thirds and colour green with green food colouring; colour remaining piece bright red using red food colouring. Roll out green sugarpaste thinly on a surface lightly sprinkled with cornflour (cornstarch). Using a holly leaf cutter, cut out 16 holly leaves (see below). Mark the veins with a knife, curve each leaf and place over lengths of dowel until dry. Shape small red berries from red sugarpaste and leave to dry. Roll out remaining red sugarpaste and cut out the letters N O E L using a small knife or alphabet cutter (see below).

Arrange the holly leaves, berries and N O E L on top of sugarpasted cake, secure with a little egg white. Measure and cut ribbon to fit cake, securing ends with stainless steel pins. Tie a bow of each colour and pin to the cake. Leave to dry.

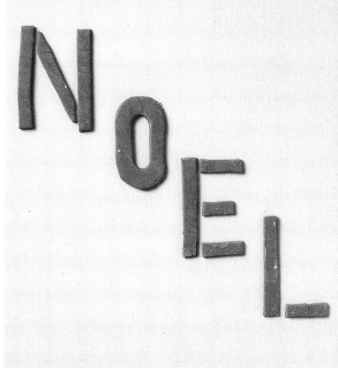

75

ROYAL ICING

This is the classic icing for wedding, Christmas and other celebration cakes. In this chapter there are detailed instructions on how to make the icing and also how to flat ice a cake. It is important to spend some time perfecting this skill as it is the basis for all further decoration. Some time is also spent discussing the nature of colour as an understanding of this can influence the design, and consequently the success of the cakes you decorate.

The peaked Christmas cake is always popular, it is quick and easy to ice and always looks effective. The wedding cake illustrates how flat icing can be the basis of further decoration, the cake is decorated entirely with sugarpaste cutout triangles so that no piping skills are required.

ROYAL ICING

To produce a beautifully royal iced cake it is essential to make a good royal icing, otherwise it is impossible to obtain a smooth coating. Everything must be spotless when making the icing as little bits that get into the icing will come to the surface on a flat coat.

Fresh egg whites or dried albumen may be used, both producing good results. A little lemon juice helps to strengthen the albumen in fresh egg whites, but care must be taken not to add too much as this will make the icing short, causing it to break during piping and it will be difficult to spread. Do not add glycerine to egg albumen as it does not set as hard as fresh egg white icing.

Adding the icing (confectioner's) sugar must be a gradual process, with plenty of mixing rather than beating during each addition of sugar, until the required consistency is reached.

Royal icing should be light and slightly glossy in texture, and should be capable of forming a peak with a fine point when a wooden spoon is drawn slowly out of the icing. This ensures that the icing will flow easily for piping or spread smoothly for coating, even though the consistencies may be different.

Royal icing made with too much sugar added too quickly will form a dull, heavy icing and be grainy in appearance. It will be difficult to work with, producing bad results. As it sets it will be chalky in appearance instead of having a sparkle. It will soon become short and break when piped.

The icing must be covered to exclude all air and prevent the surface from setting. Damp plastic wrap is a good way to seal the surface, or use an airtight container filled to the top with icing to exclude any air.

Use small quantities of icing at a time in a separate bowl from the main batch, covering with damp muslin (cheesecloth) during use. Keep the icing well scraped down; if this icing does become dry, causing hard bits, the whole batch of royal icing will not be affected.

Covering with a damp cloth is fine during short periods but if left overnight the icing will absorb all the moisture from the cloth, causing the consistency to be diluted.

If the icing is too stiff, add egg white or reconstituted egg albumen to make it softer. If the icing is too soft, gradually stir in more icing (confectioner's) sugar until the icing is of the required consistency.

CONSISTENCY

The consistency of royal icing varies for different uses. Stiff for piping, slightly softer for flat or peaked icing, and thinner for runouts.

Piping consistency: when a wooden spoon is drawn out of the icing it should form a fine, sharp point; termed stiff peak.

Flat or peaked consistency: when the spoon is drawn out of the icing it should form a fine point which curves over at the end; termed soft peak.

Runout consistency: soft peak to pipe outlines, and thick cream consistency to fill in shapes.

GLYCERINE

Glycerine may be added to royal icing provided that it is not made with egg albumen. Glycerine stops the icing from drying very hard so also makes cutting easier. Do not add glycerine to icing which is to be used for fine tube work, piped flowers or runouts.

Mix the glycerine to the finished icing and beat in. Add 8 – 10 ml (1½ – 2 teaspoons) to each 500 g (1 lb/3 Cups) icing (confectioner's) sugar.

ROYAL ICING

2 egg whites
1 ml (¼ teaspoon) lemon juice
500 g (1 lb/3 Cups) icing (confectioner's) sugar
5 ml (1 teaspoon) glycerine

Place egg whites and lemon juice into a clean bowl. Using a clean wooden spoon, stir to break up egg whites. Add sufficient icing (confectioner's) sugar and mix well to form the consistency of unwhipped cream. Continue mixing and adding small quantities of sugar every few minutes until the desired consistency has been reached, mixing well after each addition.

The icing should be smooth, glossy and light. Stir in glycerine. Do not add too much sugar too quickly as this will produce dull, heavy icing which is difficult to handle.

Allow icing to rest before using it; cover the surface with a piece of damp plastic wrap and seal well. Stir icing thoroughly before use to disperse air bubbles, then adjust the consistency if necessary.

This icing is suitable for flat or peaked icing and piping.

Makes 500 g (1 lb/3½ Cups) royal icing.

ELECTRIC MIXER METHOD

If making royal icing with an electric mixer, set at the slowest speed and use a beater. Work as for hand mixing, beating for a few seconds each time a little sugar is added. It should take about four minutes all together. Scrape the sides of the bowl frequently with the plastic scraper.

MAKING ROYAL ICING

1 *Measure the lemon juice and add it to the bowl containing the egg whites.*

2 *Sift some of the measured icing (confectioner's) sugar into the bowl.*

3 *Soft peak consistency of royal icing, ready to use for flat or peaked icing.*

4 *Sharp peak consistency of royal icing, ready for piping.*

Egg Albumen Icing

Dried powdered egg albumen may be used in place of fresh egg whites for royal icing. Simply blend the egg albumen with water and use like egg whites. Used as flat icing for tiered cakes, it sets hard enough to support the weight of the cakes.

15 ml (3 teaspoons) dried egg albumen
75 ml (5 tablespoons) tepid water
500 g (1 lb/3 Cups) icing (confectioner's) sugar, sieved

Put egg albumen into a clean bowl, gradually stir in water and blend well together until liquid is smooth and free from lumps.

Add sufficient sugar and mix well to consistency of unwhipped cream. Continue mixing and adding small quantities of sugar every few minutes until desired consistency has been reached, mixing well after each addition of sugar. The icing may be made in an electric mixer on a slow speed using a whisk, not a beater.

The finished icing should be smooth, glossy and light. Do not add too much sugar too quickly as this will produce dull, heavy icing which is difficult to handle.

Allow icing to settle before using it; cover surface with a piece of damp plastic wrap and seal well. Stir icing thoroughly before use to disperse air bubbles, then adjust the consistency if necessary.

This icing is suitable for flat or peaked icing and piping. Use double-strength dried egg albumen for runouts so that they will set hard enough to remove from the paper.

Makes 500 g (1 lb/3½ Cups) royal icing.

Royal Icing Quantity Guide

It is difficult to estimate how much royal icing will be used to ice a cake as the quantity varies according to how the icing is applied and to the thickness of layers. The design also has to be taken into account, whether it is just piping, or runouts and sugar pieces.

Cake size	Quantity of Royal Icing
13 cm (5 in) square	500 g (1 lb/3½ Cups)
15 cm (6 in) round	750 g (1½ lb/4¾ Cups)
15 cm (6 in) square	
18 cm (7 in) round	1 kg (2 lb/7 Cups)
18 cm (7 in) square	
20 cm (8 in) round	1.25 kg (2½ lb/8¾ Cups)
20 cm (8 in) square	
23 cm (9 in) round	1.5 kg (3 lb/10½ Cups)
23 cm (9 in) square	1.75 kg (3½ lb/12¼ Cups)
25 cm (10 in) round	
25 cm (10 in) square	2 kg (4 lb/14 Cups)
28 cm (11 in) round	

The best guide to follow when icing cakes is to make up the royal icing in small batches using 1 kg (2 lb/7 Cups) of icing (confectioner's) sugar. Each batch of icing made is fresh and free from any impurities which may occur when large quantities are made for one cake.

The chart provides a guide for covering each cake with two or three thin layers of flat royal icing.

Flat Icing

Royal icing cannot be applied quickly. Thin layers of icing are applied to the cake in sections and time has to be allowed in between for each to dry.

Make a quantity of royal icing to soft peak consistency and cover with a clean, damp muslin (cheesecloth) to prevent drying. Make sure the marzipan on the cake is dry and firm, then place the board and cake on a turntable.

Spread a layer of icing about 5 mm (¼ in) thick evenly over the top of the cake, remove the excess icing from the edges with a small palette knife. Remove from the turntable and place on a rigid surface.

Stand directly in front of the cake with a ruler or straight edge comfortably in both hands and pull it towards you in one steady movement to smooth the top of the cake.

If the surface is not satisfactory, spread another thin layer of icing over the cake and repeat as above until the icing is smooth.

Remove the excess icing on the side of the cake to neaten the top edge using a small palette knife. Leave to dry for at least 4 hours, or overnight, in a warm, dry place.

For a round cake, place the cake on a turntable again, spread a layer of icing 5 mm (¼ in) thick around the side of the cake. Carefully remove any excess icing from the top edge.

Place a side scraper on the side of the cake, resting on the board. Pull the side scraper with one hand while rotating the turntable with the other hand, in one continuous steady movement. The side of the cake should be completely smooth. Repeat if necessary.

Carefully pull off the scraper, which will leave a fine pull-off mark on the round cake. Using a palette knife, remove the excess icing around the top of the cake.

For a square cake, ice two opposite sides. Spread the icing onto one side, pull the scraper across to smooth. Trim off excess icing and repeat on opposite sides, allowing time in between to dry.

FLAT ICING A CAKE

1 *Remove the excess icing from the top edges of the cake.*

2 *Steadily pull the straight edge across the top of the cake in one movement to smooth the icing.*

3 *Trim away the excess icing from the top edges of the cake to neaten before drying.*

4 *Use a small palette knife to spread the side of the dry cake with icing.*

5 *Remove the excess icing from the dry icing on the top edge of the cake.*

6 *Pull the side scraper across the side of the cake. Trim away the excess icing from the top edge and corners of the cake to neaten before drying.*

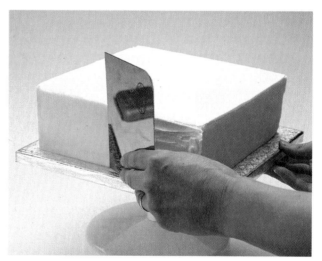

7 *The cake covered with one coat of royal icing. Dry before coating again.*

ROYAL ICED BOARD

When coating a cake or even a dummy in royal icing it is usual to coat the board as well. The board will require at least two coats of icing, to achieve a smooth finish and prevent the icing from splintering.

1 *Spread a thin layer of icing along one side of the cake board to cover evenly.*

2 *Pull the side scraper over the icing on the cake board to smooth.*

COLOURING ROYAL ICING

The overall appearance of a cake is greatly enhanced by the correct use of colour. Therefore a basic knowledge of the colour spectrum and the way in which colours complement each other is useful.

The spectrum is the range of colours as seen in a rainbow; by mixing these basic colours an infinite range of shades is obtained. When selecting colour for royal icing, take care to choose colours which look edible.

Start by adding a touch of colour to the royal icing; you can build the colour up gradually. Confectioner's colour is usually concentrated colour in liquid, dust or paste form.

The easiest colour scheme to use is monochrome, where only one colour is employed, preferably from the warmer side of the spectrum (yellow – orange – red). Use a very light shade for the base coat, a slightly stronger shade for piping shells, scrolls, etc. and then a stronger tint still for fine piping, flowers, etc.

The second method is to use contrasting or complementary colours. Here colours opposite each other on the spectrum are used, for example yellow and violet. Again, the colour should be built up from light tints, say pale yellow, for the base with a small quantity of violet added. Do not use equal amounts of the two colours or the cake will look hectic.

The most complicated colour scheme is harmony,

Colouring Royal Icing

1 *Add the food colouring to the royal icing a little at a time using a cocktail stick (toothpick).*

2 *Stir the colouring into the icing until blended.*

3 *Evenly coloured royal icing, ready to use.*

which is achieved when three to six colours next to each other on the spectrum are used. Most of the colour should be pastel, with a few darker tints.

Neutral colours, such as cream, biscuit, coffee, or chocolate can also be used to great effect. A small amount of neutral colour in any of these methods will enhance the overall appearance. White is a most effective colour to use on cakes.

When adding foliage to piped flowers, the most realistic green is obtained by adding true green to the coloured icing used for the flowers. If the colour is very deep, first make it lighter by adding white royal icing, then add the green.

Cameo colours are made by adding a touch of black to pink, green or blue.

The flowers on these practice boards illustrate monochrome, complementary and harmony colour schemes. The numbers refer to the tubes used to pipe the flowers.

SIMPLE DECORATIONS

Royal icing must be the most versatile icing; it can be smoothed onto a cake to make a perfectly flat base for decorating, or peaked and swirled to give texture to a Christmas cake. It can be piped as curves or lines from different-shaped tubes.

PEAKS AND SWIRLS

A simple way to decorate a Christmas cake is with swirls or peaks of icing with a festive centrepiece on the top. To swirl royal icing, quickly spread the top and sides of the cake as evenly as possible. Using a small palette knife, go over the surface again in circular movements to swirl the icing.

To make beautifully even peaks, the icing must be soft peak consistency. Cover the cake evenly with icing and smooth the top and sides with a palette knife. Using a small, clean palette knife dip one side into the icing. Starting from the top edge and working around the edge of the cake, press the palette knife onto the icing and pull sharply away to form a peak. Repeat to form about six peaks, then re-dip the palette knife into the icing and repeat to make peaks around the top edge.

Make the second row of peaks, in between the first row, about 1 cm (½ in) below and continue until the side is complete. Repeat to peak the top, leaving a smooth area for decoration if necessary. If the top is to be flat, flat-ice the top of a cake, then, when completely dry, peak the sides as above.

PURCHASED DECORATIONS

Flat or smooth icing takes more time and patience, but by following the step-by-step instructions and with practice, a good standard can be achieved. Once iced smoothly, the cake may be decorated with purchased decorations to suit any occasion. Tie ribbon around the side of the cake and use sugar flowers, or coloured dragées to decorate the top. Cake decorating suppliers have a vast selection to choose from.

PAINTED DESIGNS

Painting or pen designs may be applied in the same way as the sugarpaste designs. Damp is the main problem as the icing absorbs moisture, causing colours to bleed. Small runout icing plaques can be made in any shape, then the design painted on with either food colourings and a fine paintbrush, or food colouring pens. Store in a warm dry place.

COLOURED SWIRLS

Coloured icing spread into swirls over the surface is a simple way of introducing colours on to a white royal iced cake. Spread the top and sides of a marzipanned cake with white royal icing. Smooth the top and sides with a palette knife. Tint a small quantity of royal icing; use a small palette knife, dip into the tinted icing and press on to the cake and swirl. Repeat by swirling the icing, evenly spaced, over the top and sides of the cake. Try several shades of icing or contrasting colours to give a variety of swirls on the cake.

DECORATING IDEAS

A cake that has been carefully prepared and then meticulously royal iced does not need a great deal of further decoration to become a beautiful cake. However, even professional cake decorators have difficulty in perfecting the corners between the cake and the board and the area where the top and sides meet and consequently most royal iced cakes have either a piped shell at the top and bottom (for details see page 97).

FORGET-ME-NOT WEDDING CAKE

This lovely cake is made from one small and one large petal-shaped cake. It has been marzipanned and coated with three thin coats of royal icing. The shells have been piped with a No44 tube and the top row finished with loops piped with a No1 tube. Approximately 120 sugar blossoms in two shades of blue and lilac were attached to the cake with dabs

of royal icing. Tiny tear-drops in green-coloured royal icing are added to give the colour a lift. A No1 tube was used but this could have been achieved with a green-coloured food colouring pen. The elegance of the cake is reflected in the vase arrangement which consists of silk flowers and blossoms.

PEACH BLOSSOM CAKE

This cake shows the elegance of simple royal icing. The icing has been applied in three layers with 24 hours left between coats to ensure that the icing was completely dry. The shells are piped with a No5 tube. Simple blossom rosettes are repeated six times around the cake and attached with royal icing. The green-coloured tear-drops are piped with a No1 tube. The central decoration uses an opaque candle holder as the vase and uses silk tea buds, roses, marigolds and sprays of jasmine in conjunction with the ribbon to complete the arrangement. A purchased ornament could be substituted for the flowers.

RED AND GOLD CHRISTMAS CAKE

20 cm (8 in) round rich or light fruit cake, marzipanned.
25 cm (10 in) round gold cake board
1 kg (2 lb/6 Cups) royal icing
1 metre (1 yd) narrow red and gold ribbon
2 metres (2 yds) gold beading
2 gold fir trees
1 gold HAPPY CHRISTMAS emblem
1 red, gold and green holly decoration

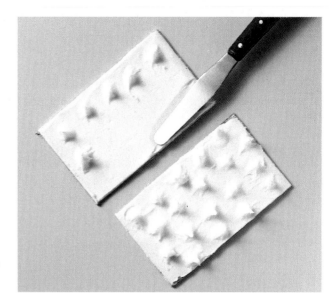

Creating peak effect royal icing.

Place marzipanned cake in centre of cake board.

Make up royal icing to soft peak consistency. Using a small palette knife, spread top and sides of cake with icing, obtaining as smooth a surface as possible. Using a clean palette knife, dip one side into the icing. Starting at the top edge and working around the edge of the cake, press palette knife on to the icing and pull sharply away to form a peak. Repeat to form about four or five peaks and re-dip the palette knife into more icing and continue until all the cake is covered in sharp peaks of royal icing.

Trim and fit ribbon and gold beading in position on side of cake while icing is damp. Tie 5 small bows and press in position around side of cake. Arrange fir trees, HAPPY CHRISTMAS emblem and holly decoration on top of cake. Leave to dry in a warm place.

SQUARE AND ROUND WEDDING CAKE

25 cm (10 in) square and a 18 cm (7 in) round rich fruit
* cakes, marzipanned and royal iced*
30 cm (12 in) square silver cake board
20 cm (8 in) round cake board
500 g (1 lb) sugarpaste
Yellow, peach and blue food colourings
1 metre (1 yd) 5 mm (¼ in) peach ribbon
1 metre (1 yd) 5 mm (¼ in) pale blue ribbon
Peach, yellow and blue silk flowers

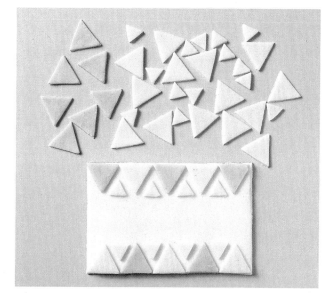

Place round cake on a round cake card, but place onto a larger board while icing for easier handling as small cake card does not show when icing and decorating has been completed.

Cut sugarpaste into three equal-sized pieces and tint one piece pale peach, one yellow and the last blue with a few drops of food colouring. Take one colour at a time, and roll out to thickness of about 3 mm (⅛ in). Cut out 15 mm (¾ in) triangles of peach and blue icing using a small triangle cutter, or cut into 15 mm (¾ in) strips and cut diagonally into triangles. Arrange alternately around top and side edges of both cakes with colours matching on top and on the sides. Cut out yellow and peach triangles and arrange around base sides of square cake. Repeat with yellow and blue triangles around base side of round cake. Cut out 5 mm (¼ in) triangles of yellow icing and arrange between peach and blue triangles on top and sides of both cakes. Cut out tiny triangles of blue icing and place between yellow and peach triangles on square cake, and tiny peach triangles between blue and yellow triangles on base of round cake.

Tie and fit peach ribbon on round cake and blue ribbon on square cake, securing with a little icing. Secure yellow and blue flowers on top and base corners of the square cake, make an arrangement in a piece of sugarpaste of peach, yellow and blue flowers. To assemble cake, place top cake carefully on centre of square cake with arrangement on top.

Sugarpaste cutouts for wedding cake.

PIPING

For many people piping is what cake decorating is all about. This chapter covers the basic skills and gives a selection of practice sheets to experiment with. It does take time to learn to pipe well, but it is a skill well worth perfecting in order to decorate classic cakes.

The featured cakes show how using only three piping tubes lovely cakes may be made; often the simpler cakes are the most effective. The cakes shown here have been marzipanned and royal iced, but further in the chapter, simple piping on sugarpaste is also shown.

BASIC PIPING

The skill of using a piping bag is worth mastering. A purchased plastic or fabric piping bag or homemade paper one, fitted with a plain or fancy piping tube, can produce shells and scrolls, bold edgings or very fine filigree work. Although piping appears to be complicated, with patience, practice and a few simple guidelines, you will discover how easy it is.

ICING

Before using any piping equipment it is essential to have the icing at the correct consistency. When a wooden spoon is drawn out of royal icing, it should form a fine but sharp point. If the icing is too stiff it will be very difficult to squeeze out of the bag; if too soft the icing will be difficult to control and the piped shapes will lose their definition.

COMMERCIAL BAGS

Piping bags made of a washable fabric are available from most cake specialist or kitchen shops. They are especially good to use if you are a beginner as they are easy to handle. Sizes vary from small to large and are ideal for piping cream, buttercream and icing onto gâteaux and simple sponge cakes. Plastic bags for piping are also available.

PAPER PIPING BAGS

These can also be purchased ready-made, but that is rather expensive as they are so simple to make. The great advantage of paper piping bags is that they can be made in advance in various sizes and can be used without a piping tube, simply by snipping the end into different shapes. After use they are thrown away, or, if the icing runs out, simply transfer the tube to a new paper bag. Choose good quality greaseproof (waxed) paper for making the bags and follow the instructions below carefully.

PIPING TUBES

These are available in a wide variety of shapes and sizes, metal and plastic, with or without a collar, so it is quite daunting to know which ones to choose. For beginners, it is advisable to start with a small selection, choosing perhaps two writing tubes, and a small, medium and large star tube. After mastering these, build up a collection for trying out new pipe designs.

Straight-sided metal tubes fit commercial bags as well as paper piping bags and give a clean, sharp result. Kept clean and stored carefully they will never need replacing and are worth the extra expense.

Some piping tubes have a collar with a screw thread at the top. This fits some commercial bags and icing syringes and has to be fitted with a screw piece. Once the bag or syringe is filled with icing, any tube with a collar may be attached so the tubes can be changed while piping. The disadvantage of these bags and tubes is that sometimes the screw is forced out of the end of the bag while piping. A collar tube is unsuitable for use with a paper piping bag.

PIPING BAGS

Well-made piping bags from greaseproof (waxed) paper are essential for good piping. Paper bags are easier to control than the plastic or metal icing syringes, and they are disposable, so do not have to be cleaned like the plastic or nylon bags.

Piping bags should never be made too large, as they will be difficult to control and the heat from your hand will change the consistency of the icing. Bags for buttercream will need to be larger than those for royal icing. If doing a lot of piping, make several bags before starting up. If piping with different coloured icing or when using different tubes, you will need several bags on hand for each one.

There are different methods for making paper piping bags. The one shown here produces bags which are a good shape and easy to use.

Making a Piping Bag

1 *Cut a piece of paper twice as long as it is wide.*

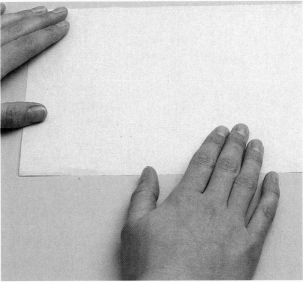

2 *Fold the paper diagonally. The points will not meet.*

3 *Cut along the fold with a sharp knife to make two right-angle triangles.*

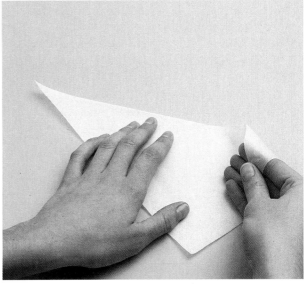

4 *Lay the triangle flat with the right angle facing you and fold the corner inwards.*

5 *Place the corner on the point of the right angle, making a cone.*

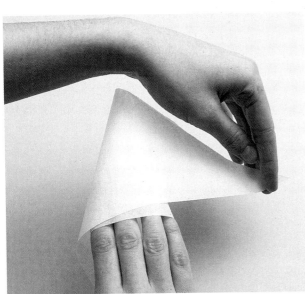

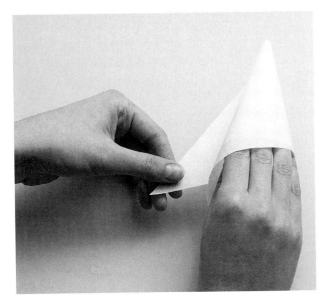

6 *Put your fingers in the cone to hold it and bring the other corner over it.*

7 *Wrap the corner around the cone twice so that the points meet.*

8 *Slide the three points together to tighten the bag.*

9 *Fold the top point into the bag. If piping without a tube, fill the bag now.*

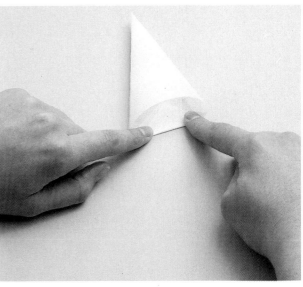

10 *If using a piping tube, cut off the tip of the bag with scissors and insert the tube..*

FILLING THE BAG

1 *Hold the bag in your hand or place on the table and hold the point. Scoop up some icing with a palette knife and place in the bag.*

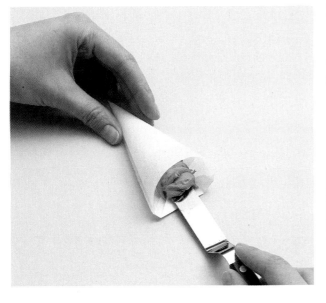

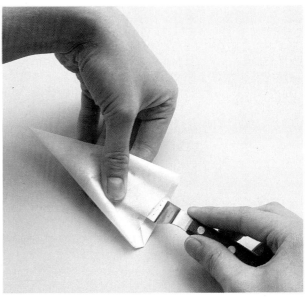

2 *Hold the top of the bag down and gently pull out the palette knife.*

3 *Fold the points of the bag towards the centre.*

4 *Fasten by folding the top of the bag over twice.*

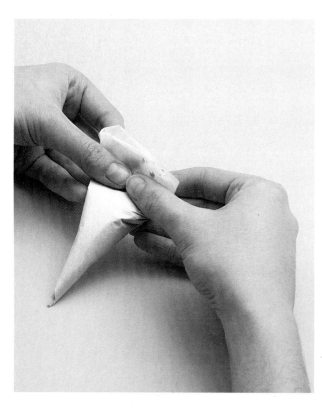

SIMPLE PIPING

Piping is the obvious choice when decorating a cake, but it is easy to be discouraged by complicated designs. Begin with these simple designs and practise until you are proficient, then you may apply these skills to decorating a cake.

Choose just a simple star tube and fit it into a paper piping bag to pipe swirls, scrolls and shells. Tint some buttercream or royal icing of sharp peak consistency with a small amount of food colouring. Half-fill the piping bag, fold down the top and squeeze the icing to the end of the tube. Place the icing tube just onto the surface of the cake. Pipe a swirl of icing in a circular movement, stop pressing the bag and pull up sharply to break the thread. Repeat to pipe swirls around the top edge and base of the cake if desired.

To pipe a star shape from the same tube, hold the bag straight above the surface of the cake. Press the icing out to form a star on the edge of the cake, then stop pressing and pull up sharply to break the icing; repeat to make a neat border.

To pipe scrolls hold the piping bag at an angle so that the piping tube is almost on its side.

Pipe some icing on the top edge of the cake to secure the scroll. Pipe outwards in a circular movement and return the piping tube to the edge of the cake. Stop pressing the bag and break off the icing. Repeat again, but pipe the icing inwards to the cake in a circular movement, then return the piping tube just to the edge. This is piping scrolls curving inwards and outwards. For a different design, pipe the scrolls in one direction only.

To pipe shells, hold the piping bag at an angle to the cake so that the piping tube is almost on its side. Press out some icing and secure to the surface of the cake, press gently, move the tube forward, then move it slowly up, over and down almost like a rocking movement. Stop pressing and break off the icing by pulling the tube towards you. Repeat, piping the icing onto the end of the first shell to make a shell edging.

To pipe lines, fit the piping bag with a plain writing tube and fill with icing. Pipe a line of icing, securing the end to the surface of the cake. Continue to pipe the icing just above the surface of the cake, allowing the threads to fall in a straight or curved line. Stop pressing the bag and sharply break off the line of icing.

To pipe leaves, cut the end of the paper piping bag into an inverted V. Fill with icing and press the icing to the end of the bag. Place the end on the surface of the cake. Press out the icing to form a leaf shape, press harder to make a larger leaf, then sharply break off the icing. Repeat to make a pretty border, or just to decorate flowers or to make a design.

To pipe a star border, use paper piping bag, trim the end into a W shape and fill with icing. Place the pointed end on the surface of the cake at an angle and pipe out a star shape. Repeat, piping stars close together to form a border design.

To pipe basket-weave, fit a paper piping bag with a ribbon or basket-weave tube. Pipe a vertical line from the top of the cake to the bottom. Pipe 2 cm (¾ in) lines across the vertical line at intervals the width of the tube. Pipe another vertical line of icing on the edge of the horizontal lines, then pipe short lines of icing in between the spaces across the vertical line to form a basket-weave. Repeat until the cake is completely covered.

SIMPLE PIPING

1 *To pipe a star, hold the piping bag vertically and press out the icing, stop pressing to stop the flow of icing and lift sharply.*

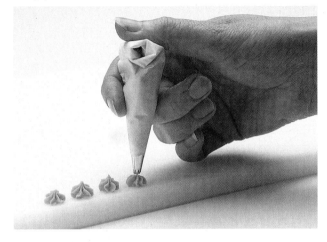

2 *The same stars piped from an icing syringe, try both methods to see which you find easiest.*
Using a larger tube a bigger star can be piped.

3 *To pipe a shell border, hold the bag at an angle and pipe a row of shells. Stop pressing the bag to finish each shell before placing the next.*

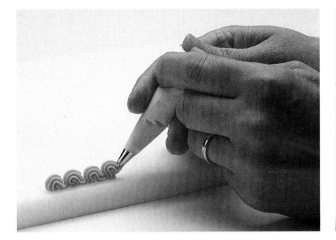

4 *Hold a paper piping bag fitted with a star tube at an angle to pipe individual scrolls. Stop pressing the bag and pull off sharply to finish each scroll.*

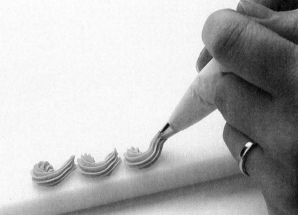

Writing tubes	Star and Shell Tubes	Petal and Basketweave Tubes
No4 writing tube	No6 star tube	No56 flower or petal tube
No3 writing tube	No15 star tube	No59 flower or petal tube
No2 writing tube	No9 star tube	No23 basketweave tube
	No12 star tube	
	No42 shell tube	
	Nno44 shell tube	
	No5 shell tube	
	No7 star tube	
	No8 star tube	

5 Use a paper piping bag snipped into a V-shape to pipe these leaf shapes.

6 To pipe basket-weave, pipe a vertical line of icing, then overpipe horizontal lengths of icing at evenly spaced intervals. Pipe a second vertical line of icing over the short horizontal lines, then repeat the pattern.

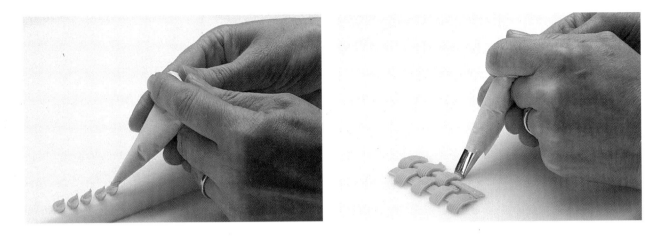

TASSEL AND SHELL BORDERS

1 Use a star tube for tassel borders. Lean over the cake and pipe a rosette on the board. Bring the tube towards you to a height of 3 cm (1¼ in), decreasing the pressure to make the tassel shape.

2 If wished, pipe drop loops in different colours from one tassel to the next. Use a fine tube. The design shown here features four colours but would work well in one or two.

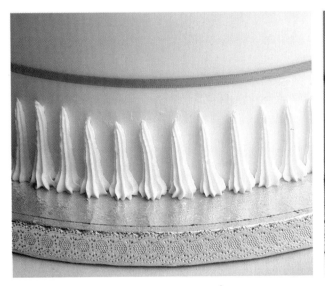
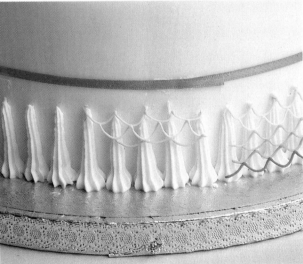

Any shell tube can be used for this technique. Hold the tube at a 45 degree angle to the cake. Squeeze to form a shell, pull to the right (to the left if you are left-handed) while releasing pressure. Hold the tube at this position to pipe the next shell.

The shell border is overpiped with a circle using a No00 tube.

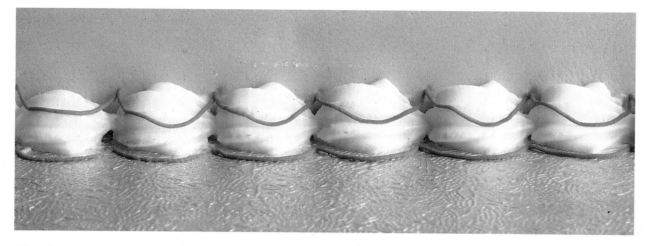

Pipe the shells vertically with the points at the top. Drop loops from the top of alternate points.

LINES

To give strength to icing used for these techniques add 15 ml (3 tsp) of powdered egg white to 60 ml (2 floz/ ¼ Cup) water and 500 g (1 lb/3 ½ Cups) icing. Beginners should start with linework to get the feel of the icing and bag and to train their hands in getting the correct pressure. Press, stop pressing, pull down. This will become a natural action. Lines may be overpiped and built up for more elaborate effects.

Fine and bold straight lines can be piped with any writing tube. Place the tube on the cake or practice board, press slowly and evenly and hold in position about 2.5 cm (1 in) above line required. Let the icing drop into place for about three-quarters of the line. Stop pressing before the end of the line, as enough icing will be left in the action to ease the line onto the cake. Touch down gently taking the tube off. You will have a clean line without a large blob at the end.

PRACTICE SHEETS

Use icing at full peak with air bubbles paddled out. Sit comfortably holding the icing bag easily in your hand. Relax your hand and arm. Start by piping straight lines following the practice board on page 101. The lighter lines are piped with a No1 tube, the darker lines with a No0. Hold tube in an upright position; press, stop pressing, pull down. This sequence is used for most piping actions.

1 *Scroll piped with No46, overpiped with white in No1 and graduated dot piped in mauve with No0.*

2 *Plain scroll and dot.*

3 *Two scrolls piped facing.*

4 *Facing scrolls plus overpiping and trellis made with No0 tube.*

5 *Scroll plus overpiping with No59. To pipe the frill at the base, pleat as you pipe with the thick side of the tube touching the cake, fine side outwards.*

6 *Extending star piped with No46. Press, stop pressing, pull out. Pipe star with No43 tube under large ones. Overpipe first with white using No1, then mauve with No0. Pipe loop from small star, then loop from every other large star.*

7 *Extending star piped with No46 with star piped with No43 at base. The loop is piped with a No0 tube.*

8 *Bottom border design only piped with No46; press, stop pressing, pull down. Loops piped with No0 tube.*

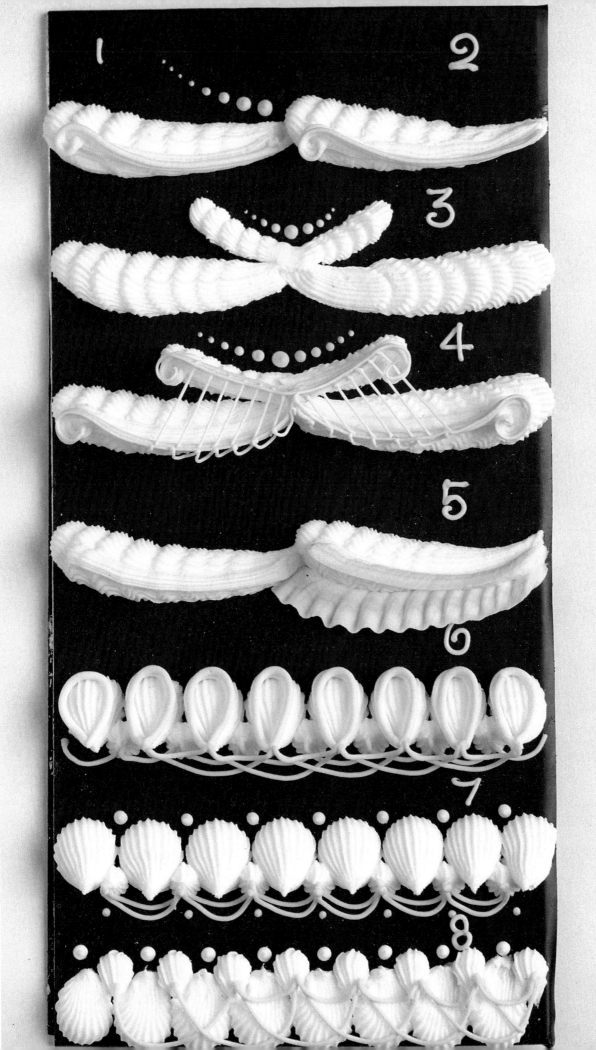

1 *Practise piping dots in sets of three using a No1 tube. This exercise gives spacing practice.*

2 *Next pipe the graduated dots, pressing less as the dot gets smaller.*

3 *Shells are piped with a No46 tube.*

4 *Shell overpiped once in white with No1.*

5 *Shell overpiped with No1 and No0 tubes.*

6 *Shell overpiped with No59 tube; thick side of the tube touching shell, fine side upright.*

7 *Heart piped with No46 and overpiped with No59 with dots added.*

8 *Heart shape shell overpiped with No1 tube.*

9 *Heart shape shell plus over-piping in white with No1 and overpiping in mauve with No0.*

10 *Heart shape shell piped with No46.*

11 *Heart shape shell with centre overpiped with No59.*

12 *Plain scroll piped with No46. To pipe, start fairly small, build up in centre and then ease off to finish.*

13 *Scroll with overpiped lines.*

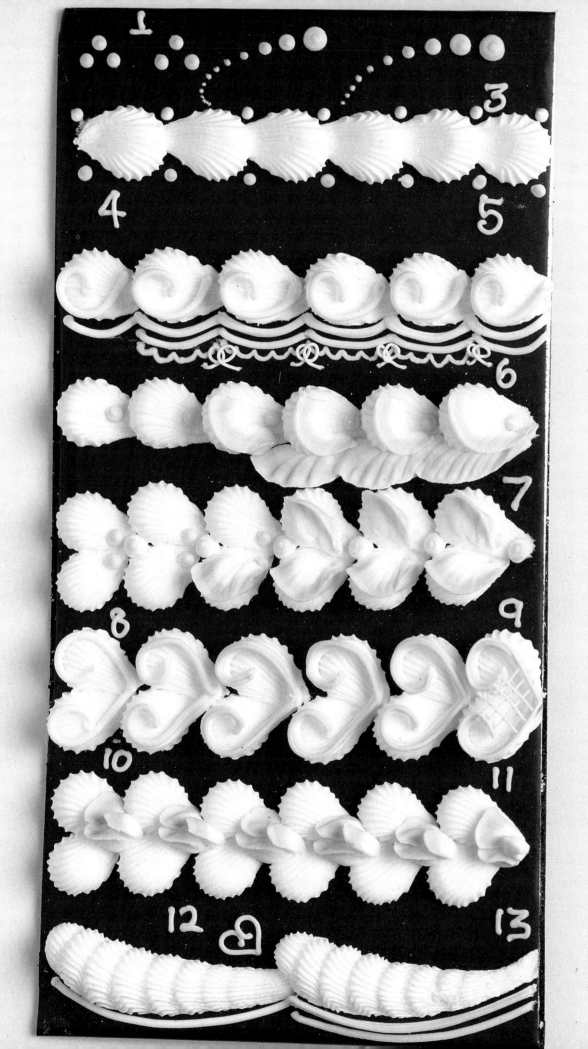

DECORATING IDEAS

BUTTERCREAM SPONGE

Spread the top and sides of a 20 cm (8 in) round sponge with 250 g (8 oz/1 Cup) of buttercream. Smooth the surface with a small palette knife dipped in hot water. Tint some buttercream with a few drops of orange food colouring and fill a piping bag fitted with a small star tube. Pipe alternate inwards and outwards scrolls around the top and bottom edges of the cake. Mark a 6 cm (2½ in) circle in the centre using a plain cutter and pipe scrolls around the outside of the marked circle. Pipe groups of three stars of icing at intervals around the side and top of the cake.

BASKET CAKE

Make a pudding basin (bowl) sponge cake, flavour 250 g (8 oz/1 Cup) of buttercream with cocoa powder and spread thinly on the cake; place on a small cake board. Fit a paper piping bag with a basket or ribbon tube and fill with icing. Fold down the top and pipe a basket-weave design all around the cake until completely covered. Pipe a shell edging around the base and the top edge using the same piping tube. Fold a 20 cm (8 in) length of foil into a narrow strip. Wrap 1 cm (½ in) wide ribbon just overlapping around the strip of foil to cover, then secure the end with sticky tape. Bend to form a handle, press carefully into the top of the cake and tie a bow on the handle. Fill the centre of the basket with sugar and chocolate eggs, or sugar flowers.

BUNNY CAKE

Make a sponge cake in a novelty tin (pan) following the manufacturer's instructions. Leave for at least four hours before decorating. Cover the cake board with a layer of green-coloured sugarpaste, then place the rabbit in the centre of the board. Colour some buttercream pink, then pipe lines to define the legs and mouth using a No3 tube. Cut out ovals of pink sugarpaste for the nose and the insides of the ears and fix in position with a little boiled water. To make the rabbit's eyes, colour some sugarpaste pale blue and fix in place with boiled water. Paint in the pupils with black liquid food colouring. Make a carrot from some sugarpaste coloured orange, and score its undersurface with a sharp knife to make indentations. Using a No13 tube and uncoloured buttercream, pipe stars over the whole of the rabbit's body, working in neat horizontal rows so that the surface of the cake cannot be seen. Then, using pink buttercream, pipe in a pink tail made from rows of stars. Finish the rabbit by fixing a sugar flower between its ears and giving it two front teeth made from white buttercream.

CHRISTMAS TREE CAKE

Cut a sponge or Madeira cake into a Christmas tree shape with a small, sharp knife. You can cut the cake freehand, but you may find it easier to draw the required shape on a sheet of paper, then pin this template on the cake and cut around it. With a palette knife, spread the thick white glacé icing over the top of the cake and leave for five minutes to set slightly. Then with the No2 tube and runny green glacé icing, pipe lines down the length of the cake, about 2 cm (¾ in) apart. Before the icing has set, draw lines at right angles over the green icing with the skewer. Decorate with gold, silver and red dragées. Insert the No8 star tube into a piping bag and fill it with green buttercream. Pipe rows of stars along the sides of the cake. Place one ribbon rosette at the top of the tree and three along its base to complete the decoration.

105

RIBBON CAKE

*20 cm (8 in) square fruit cake, marzipanned and royal iced
in lemon on a 25 cm (10 in) silver drum board*
500 g (1 lb/3 ½ Cups) royal icing
Coffee-coloured food colouring
1 ½ metres (1 ½ yds) 1 cm (½ in) coffee-coloured ribbon
24 iced roses in deep lemon
16 silver rose leaves

Lay the ribbon over the cake as shown. Attach the
ribbons to the centre base on all sides securing with
dots of royal icing. Cut the ribbon ends into a V
shape.

Colour the icing to a rich coffee colour, then with
No3 tube make rows of dots on the sides of the cake
in the V shape that is created by the ribbon. Pipe
rows of dots on top beside the ribbon.

Using a No44 tube, pipe a shell edge on the top
stopping where the ribbon crosses the edge, see
photograph. Attach the purchased roses and leaves
with icing.

HEART-SHAPED CAKE

*25 cm (10 in) heart-shaped rich or light fruit cake,
marzipanned and royal iced in peach on a 30 cm (12 in)
silver drum board*
750 g (1 ½ lbs/5 ¼ Cups) royal icing
Silver balls
Silk flowers

Make a 20 cm (8 in) heart template as a piping guide,
pipe a line of white icing with a No3 tube then
overpipe with a No2 tube. Pipe two more lines inside
the first with a No2 and then a No1 tube.

Using a No44 star tube, pipe a line of stars all the
way around the top and bottom edges and centre
of the sides of the cake. Then, using a No2 tube,
pipe a line following shape of top and bottom
stars, then pipe a loop from star to star allowing the
loops to drop down evenly as shown. Place a silver
ball in the centre of each star before the icing sets.

Arrange the silk flowers and position on the cake
securing with a little royal icing.

Detail of cake showing the ribbon and piping.

Close-up of cake side showing the linked star design.

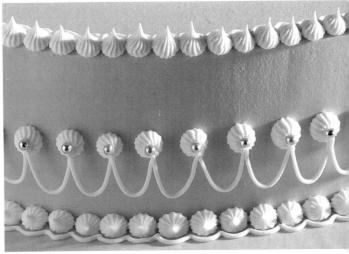

106

1ST BIRTHDAY CAKE

20 cm (8 in) hexagonal fruit cake
750 g (1½ lb) marzipan
750 g (1½ lb) sugarpaste
25 cm (10 in) hexagonal board
Red, yellow, green, blue and black food colourings
Clear spirit (gin or vodka)
125 g (4 oz/⅔ Cup) royal icing
1½ metres (1¼ yards) 3 mm (⅛ in) coloured ribbon to
   match colours of tortoise

Cover cake with marzipan and sugarpaste and place in centre of board.

Colour small amounts of sugarpaste with red, blue, green and yellow, kneading colour in well to avoid streaking. Trace patterns of tortoise (page 251) and number. Cut out each individual section. Roll out the coloured paste, place the templates on the appropriate colours and cut out the shapes with a modelling knife. Assemble as shown in the picture. Moisten the underside of the coloured sections with clear spirit. Place on the cake. With a fine brush and black food colouring, paint in facial features.

Mark a line around the cake approximately 4 cm (1½ in) from the board. Using a No43 tube, pipe a large bulb of icing at the base of the cake; without removing the tip of the tube and maintaining the even pressure, draw the line of icing up as far as the guideline (see step-by-step picture). Pipe these columns all around the cake, evenly spaced about 2 cm (¾ in) apart. Allow to dry thoroughly.

With a No2 tube, touch the tip of the tube to the top of the rope, hold the tube level with the top and let out a thread of icing allowing it to drop slightly to form a loop. Attach to the next column. Repeat all round the cake. Pipe a second row below the first and repeat loops to the bottom of the cake. It is easier to work with the cake at eye-level, placed on a turntable.

Wrap narrow bands of coloured ribbon around the cake attaching with dots of icing at the points of the hexagon. Leave narrow gaps between ribbons. Pipe blue dots below the first band of ribbon at the top of the piping. Pipe graduated lines of dots in gaps between ribbons.

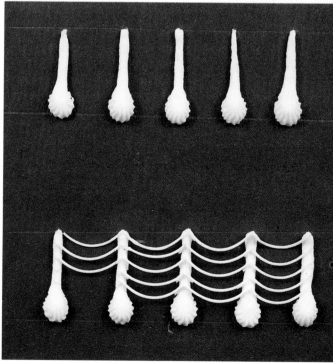

107

PIPING TECHNIQUES

This chapter builds on the skills learnt in the preceding chapter. More complicated piping skills are covered such as pressure piping which can be used to create small decorations in semi-relief; embroidery work which is so useful particularly for side designs on wedding cakes and cornelli work which is so simple but so very useful. In addition simple piped flowers are covered as well as runout techniques, both of which look more complicated than they really are.

The lace wedding cake featured here uses piped line work and cornelli work to create a classic cake. Traditionally the top tier of the wedding cake is kept to make the Christening cake and this one has here been overpiped in pink for the occasion. Overpiping in blue would work equally well. Unless you anticipate using the Christening cake within a year of the wedding it is best to make the cake afresh, but it is still a nice idea to remind the guests of the earlier celebration by reproducing the wedding cake design.

109

PRESSURE PIPING

This is a method for building up three-dimensional piped pictures by increasing or decreasing the amount of pressure. Trace the design and transfer it to a cake or plaque. Look at the original and decide which part should appear to be furthest away, and start piping with that part. Use a bag with a No2 tube, then add details with a smaller tube. Build up the picture, increasing the pressure for parts which need to stand out.

BOOTIES AND BIRDS

1   *With a No1 tube press, stop pressing, pull down. Press again to form side of bootie.*

2   *Pipe a second bootie.*

3   *Pipe two lines around top. Overpipe with pink.*

4   *Booties piped on ribbon bow.*

5   *Birds on ribbon bows.*

PRESSURE-PIPED RABBITS

1   *Pipe a bulb for the head.*

2   *Pipe the body. This is a large shell piped from the bottom upwards.*

3   *The ears and top part of the legs are piped on both using shell shapes.*

4   *Pipe in the feet, arms and the whiskers with a No0 tube. The body is textured with a fine paint-brush, either while piping or when the rabbit is finished. These rabbits can also be piped in miniature.*

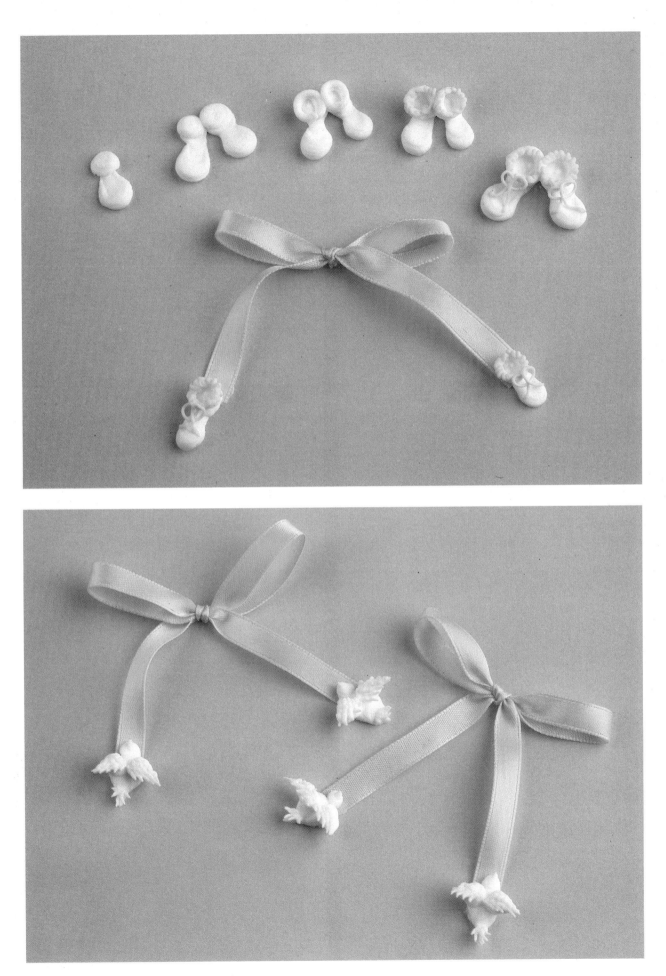

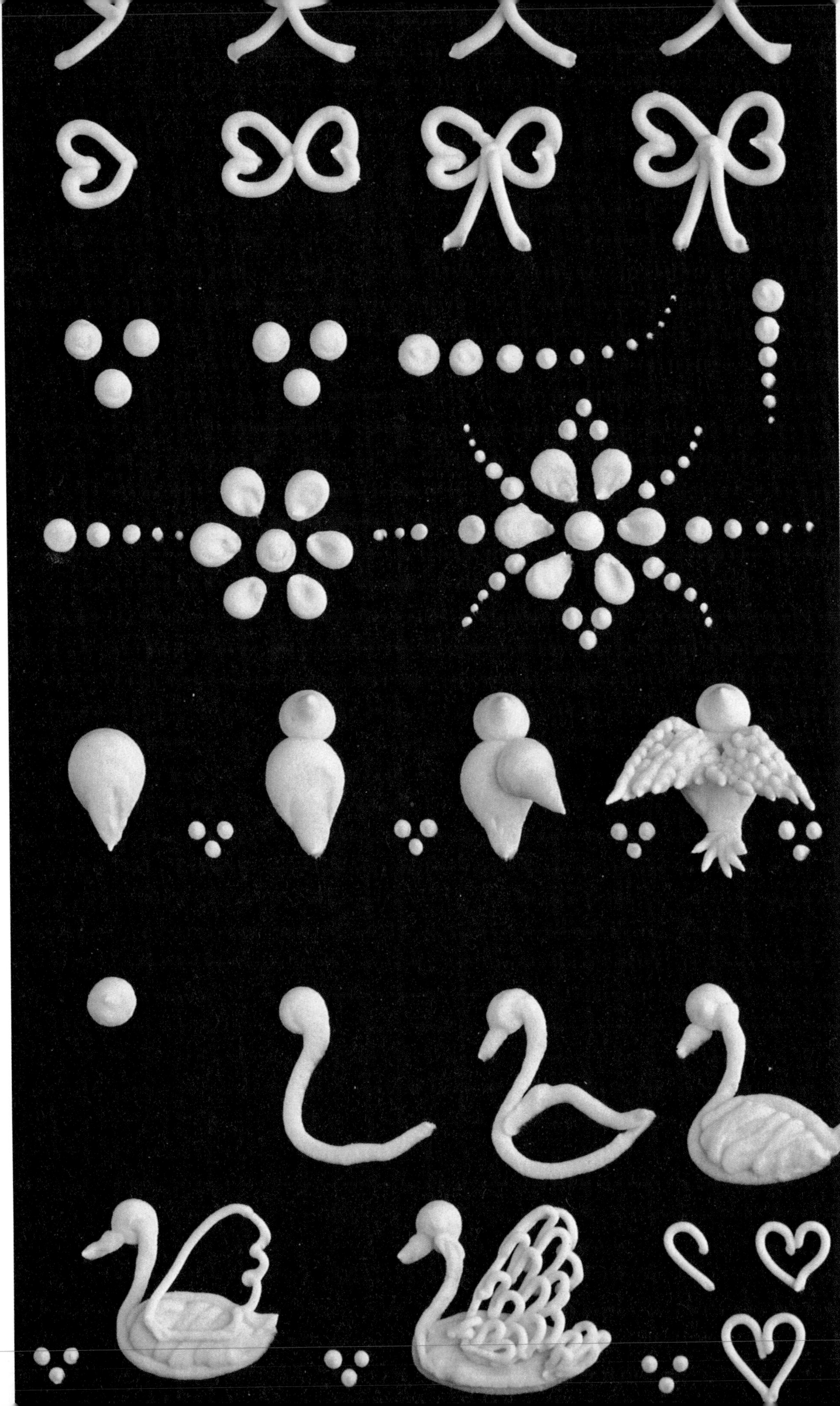

PRACTICE SHEET

Dot flowers: Press, stop pressing, pull down to form a pear shape for each petal.

Birds: Press to form a pear shape for the body; press, stop pressing, pull up to form head and beak. Press, stop pressing, pull out to form wing, repeat for other side. Press wings and tail.

Swan: Pipe head and pull an S line to form breast and neck. Pipe arch for back and tail, add beak. Fill in body. Pipe an outline for the wing, then pipe loops for feathers.

Hearts: Pipe left loop then right loop. Join at the bottom.

Heart: Press, stop pressing, pull down. Pipe left side first, then right.

Lovers' knot: Press, loop left side round, press, loop right side round.

Lovers' knot heart style: Press out a small heart sideways, then another the other way. Pipe two lines downwards.

Dots: Press, stop pressing, ease off. For graduated dots press less as they get smaller. For the smallest dot the tube should just barely touch the cake.

CORNELLI WORK

Cornelli work looks attractive worked in a contrasting colour and is useful for hiding a poor cake surface. Cornelli work is simply a continuous wavy line piped with a No0 or No00 writing tube. Work on a small area at a time keeping the line equidistant from any others. Bend the line up and down and from side to side, varying it all the time. If you find this difficult, practise by drawing a line on paper first, and then piping over it.

RUNOUTS

Runout, or flood work, is a method used to make figures, plaques, collars and borders. Any picture or design may be copied for a runout. Beginners should start with a simple shape.

Favourite children's cakes are made using runout characters copied from books or comics. Cakes with figures taken from birthday cards are fun for older children. Cuttings from newspapers or even lettering can be made in runout icing.

Runout icing is made by taking the required quantity of royal icing and breaking it down to a flowing consistency by adding small amounts of cold water, a little at a time. Paddle away the bubbles with a knife before adding the water. If the mixture becomes too runny, add some firm royal icing; if still too firm, add more water. The right consistency will come with practice and time.

With a spoon, fill a large bag about half full with runout icing. Fold in the top of the bag firmly to prevent icing oozing out, then cut a small piece from the point the size of a tube No0 to No3. The larger the surface to be filled in, the larger the hole.

Place the chosen picture under the cellophane or roasting wrap pinned well down on a soft drawing or macramé board. Outline with a fine tube. Pipe unbroken lines around the picture, then flood.

Pipe the background first, leave to dry for about 30 minutes; then pipe the foreground. A crust forms on the icing, so the outline of the foreground will be thicker giving the picture depth.

The sections you want to stand out are flooded last. Work in stages so that the picture dries out in sections for painting.

113

When flooding keep the point of the bag submerged in the royal icing. Take care at all times to work right up to the piped edge or border, filling in all corners and edges to eliminate air bubbles. Work icing in a circular movement to keep it even. Should air bubbles appear, break immediately with a pointed tool and pull to the edge of the design.

PIPED OUTLINE LEAVES

1 *Prepare a template of a holly leaf. Place a piece of waxed paper over the template, securing with masking tape or small dots of icing at each corner. Pipe the outline and centre vein with green icing and a No1 or No2 tube, depending on the size of the leaf. Allow the leaves to dry flat or over curved formers.*

RUNOUT LEAVES

1 *Follow the instructions for piped outline leaves, then flood in with green runout icing. The centre vein may be omitted or retained. If the vein is retained and the flooding of each side of the leaf is carried out separately, allow the first half to skin over before flooding in the other side.*

2 *Allow the leaves to dry flat or over curved formers. Apply green and brown tones using a dry paintbrush and edible petal dust, or an aerograph spray. The leaves could also be painted with food colour to give more detail.*

CAROL SINGER

1 *To make the runout figure, trace the outline onto drawing paper. Place a piece of waxed paper over the tracing and outline using a No1 tube.*

2 *Flood in each section separately. Allow sections to skin over before flooding in adjacent sections.*

3 *Continue flooding in until the figure is complete. Let dry.*

4 *Paint detail on the figure with a fine paintbrush and food colouring.*

PIPED FLOWERS

Piped flowers can be made in many different varieties, shapes and sizes. Flowers can either be piped onto flower nails, or onto squares of waxed paper stuck onto the worksurface. Cut several 2.5 cm (1 in) squares of wax paper before beginning. Flowers are piped with a petal tube, and these are available in right-handed and left-handed versions. Piping perfect flowers takes a lot of practice to know how to maintain the correct pressure and learn when to release the pressure. The icing must be fairly firm, so that the flowers hold their shape.

1 *Place a square of waxed paper on the worksurface. Place the petal tube in the end of a bag and fill with stiff royal icing. The thicker end of the tube should always be towards the centre of the flower. Start off piping, using your wrist to give the flow to the petals, and keeping an even pressure. Pipe a tight horseshoe shape.*

2 *Rotate the waxed paper and pipe the second petal.*

3 *Rotate the waxed paper and pipe the third petal. You should have covered two-thirds of the circumference of the flower. If not, the petals are either too fat or too thin.*

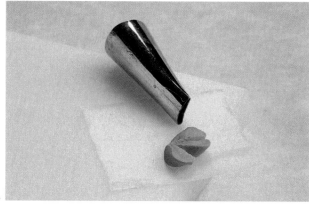

4 *Rotate the waxed paper and pipe the fourth petal.*

5 *Rotate the waxed paper and pipe the fifth petal, release pressure and carefully lift the bag away. Pipe a small dot in the centre using a contrasting colour and a small tube. This is a basic piped blossom.*

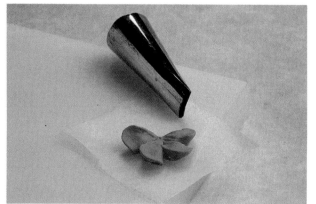

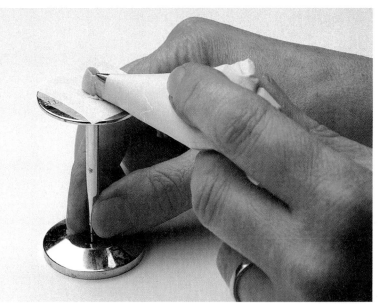

SIMPLE FLOWERS PIPED ON NAILS

1 *To pipe a rose secure a piece of greaseproof or waxed paper to the rose nail with a bead of icing. Pipe the centre using a petal tube on the paper and turning the nail at the same time to form a cone shape. Keep the piping tube upright and the thick end of the tube at the base.*

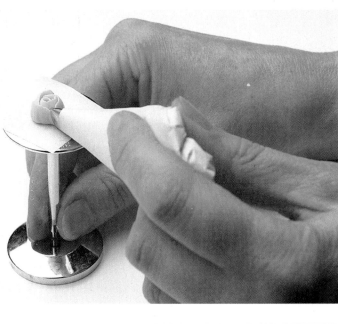

2 *Pipe the third petal around the centre petals turning the nail at the same time as pressing the bag.*

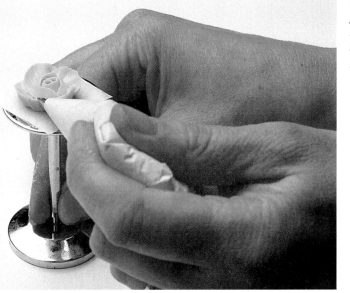

3 *Hold the piping bag at an angle to pipe the final petals. To pipe a rose bud, start with the centre cone, then pipe around more petals until the bud is the size required.*

BUTTERCREAM CATTLEYA ORCHID

The cattleya orchid here and all of the buttercream flowers on the following pages have been piped with a No59 tube, but another petal tube could also be used. The orchid can either be made as shown, with the base petals a different colour from the tongue, or by the colour flow method, using two colours in the same bag.

1   *Take a piece of waxed paper and mark a centre dot with a pencil. To make the first petal, pipe a shell about 4 cm (1 ½ in) long from the dot to the outside edge with a petal tube. Pipe a flat line of buttercream up either side of the shell. Pipe two more petals in the arrangement shown, exactly as for the first petal.*

2   *Pipe the upper two halves of the frilled petals. Keep the thick end of the tube towards the centre and move your hand backwards and forwards to make a frilled edge. Make the bottom halves in the same way. Pull a small paintbrush down the centre of each petal to make the vein. Refrigerate for 10 minutes.*

3   *For the tongue, pipe three horseshoe shapes upside-down as you look on towards the top petal. Pipe a frilly edge around the outside of each one.*

4   *Pipe the column in the centre of the tongue using a small bag and a No2 tube. Mark two holes in the end of the column with a cocktail stick (toothpick). When the orchid is dry, paint on any additional colouring with oil-based food colouring or petal dust.*

PHILIPPINE WIRED FLOWERS

These small Philippine-style flowers make lovely additions to both sugar and fabric flower sprays. They are most useful for softening sprays, and for enlarging or adding height to top ornaments.

Bend 28- or 30-gauge covered wire into soft curves. This must be done before piping the flowers, as the flowers might break or fall off if the wire is bent afterwards. Place the bent wire on wax paper.

The flowers and foliage are piped with a No1 tube. Copy the ones shown here, or pipe similar tiny flowers copied from fresh flowers. Leave to dry thoroughly.

Peel carefully off the wax paper, starting from the end of the wire. If double-sided flowers are required, turn over and pipe on the other side.

PIPED BASKETS

Piped baskets may be made in any shape using a basket nail or a small round object. Dust the mould with a little icing (confectioner's) sugar then cover with rolled out sugarpaste in the same colour as the basket. Different size tubes may be used depending on the size of the weave. Use the same firm icing as for piped flowers. The downward line should be one size smaller than the cross line. Two colours can be used. Babies' cradles can be made in the same way.

1   *Cover the basket nail or pot with a little sugarpaste or flower paste (see page 172).*

2   *Starting at the bottom, pipe basket-weave – a long line with short lines crossing it. Pipe round the base of the basket, then the sides. Keep the tube in the same position and pipe loops to join the coloured lines.*

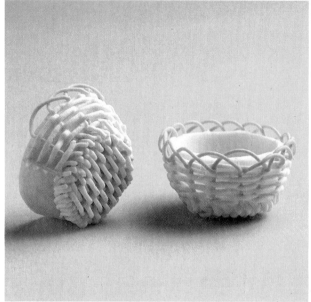

3   *Leave to dry overnight. Take the basket off the mould. If it doesn't come off easily it needs more drying time. Insert green sugarpaste.*

4   *The handle can be milliner's wire covered with piping. Stick it to the bottom of the basket with icing. After 24 hours when the icing is set the basket can be picked up by the handle.*

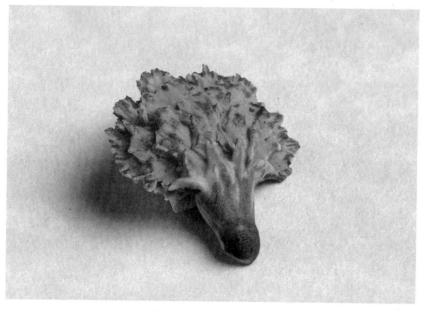

VIOLET

This is just a variation on the basic piped blossom. Study the shape and pipe with violet-coloured icing.

CARNATION

Pipe the round basic shape. Using a fine, moist paintbrush, feather the ends of the petals while the icing is still wet. Pipe calyx when slightly dry.

DAISY

Use the same technique as for the basic blossom, but go up and down instead of making a horseshoe, and make more petals.

MORE BUTTERCREAM FLOWERS

CARNATION

Pipe a ring of buttercream, keeping the narrow end towards the outside, and moving the tube back and forth to give a frilled edge. Pipe single frilled petals to fill the centre, working in a clockwise direction. Refrigerate until firm. Carefully remove the flower from the waxed paper, turn over and make a calyx by piping a pulled-up star with a No7 tube.

DAFFODIL

Pipe the six petals, then pull a small paintbrush down the centre of each one and pinch the ends to make a slight point. Refrigerate for a few minutes. Pipe a circle for the trumpet by holding the tube upright with the thicker end at the base and pulling as you pipe to make the frilled edge. Pipe some green stamens in the centre of the trumpet.

ARUM LILY

Pipe a petal-shape in white buttercream. Pipe a yellow pistil with a No3 tube. Using the white icing, join a strip to the petal shape, fold either side over to cover the base of the pistil. Dry, then pipe on a green calyx.

BRIAR ROSE

Pipe as for the blossom, but make the petals heart-shaped by flicking your wrist back and forth at the top of each petal. Pipe some yellow stamens in the centre, and dust with green petal dust.

FORGET-ME-NOT

Place royal icing in the bag, white on the broad side of the tube and blue on the narrow side.

Hold the bag horizontally with the broad side of the tube as the centre of the nail. Squeeze the bag and move your right hand in an anti-clockwise direction while your left hand turns the nail in an anti-clockwise direction. Move through almost one-quarter of a circle. Stop the pressure and finish with a slicing movement towards the centre of the flower. The second and subsequent petals overlap the preceding one and the fifth petal is piped over the first. Finish with a small piped yellow dot.

NARCISSUS

Pipe white petals with the tube flat as for forget-me-not, but move tube out and in again to get the correct length. Pipe the first three petals an even distance apart. Pipe the next three petals in the gaps. Pinch each petal at the end or stroke it with a paintbrush. Pipe the centre with a No1 tube. First pipe a spiral around it to form the trumpet. Finish with a zig-zag line at the top. Paint with orange food colour.

PRIMROSE

Use pale yellow royal icing. Follow the instructions for piping the forget-me-not, but halfway around each petal move the tube in towards the centre and then out again. When the flowers are dry, paint or petal dust the centres a darker yellow. Pipe a white dot in each centre.

APPLE BLOSSOM

Pipe as forget-me-not, but finish with piped green dots.

MARKING OUT THE DESIGN

PRICKING

Trace the design onto tracing paper. Place this on the cake or plaque and carefully prick the outline with a pin. Do not mark too many details as this will be confusing and these small features can easily be copied when the design is almost finished. This method is not suitable for hard surfaces.

PENCIL TRACING

The usual method of tracing is to turn over the design, re-draw on the back with a sugarcraft pen, or with a non-toxic pastel pencil, place this side on the surface to be decorated and trace again over the outline. This leaves the fine lines of the pattern on the surface. Do not use very heavy lines as these will be difficult to conceal and could smudge. Small pieces of outline embroidery which are mainly used to decorate the sides of a cake or scattered around a large decoration to give a softening effect are usually done freehand with a No0 or 00 tube. The focal points of the design may be pricked out with a pin, this will ensure that the side motifs look uniform even though there may be some slight variations. The icing tube should gently scrape the surface as the icing is squeezed out using an even pressure and should be held rather like a pen. Fresh soft icing which has been well beaten should be used, this should flow easily without needing too much pressure.

Flower embroidery side designs based on dots and pulled dots.

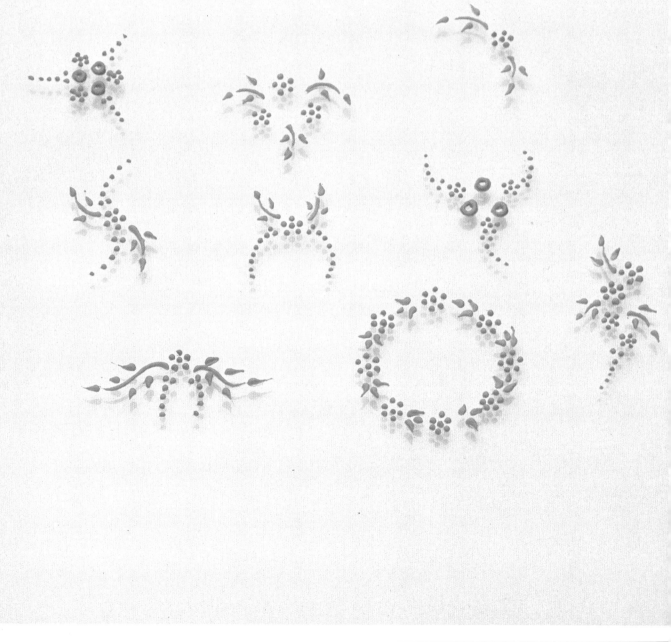

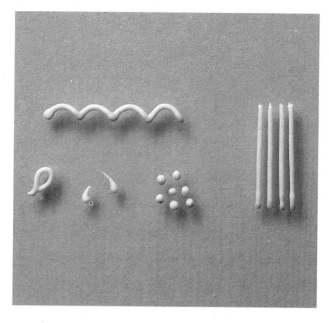

BASIC EMBROIDERY

1. Dots: Piped dots should not have points so keep the icing soft. Just touch the tube to the cake surface, apply pressure and stop when the dot is the required size.

2. Pulled dots: Pipe dot, then pull the tube away to the side.

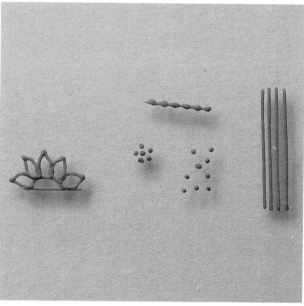

3. Leaf shape: Start at the point, curve around and finish neatly. The sides can be curved slightly or more deeply as in a teardrop.

4. Flowers: These can be five dots piped around one dot; pulled dots around one dot; or leaf shapes piped in a circle, pointing in or out.

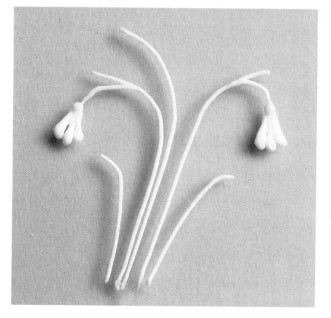

5. Snowdrops: Pipe three teardrops with a bulb at the top.

DECORATING IDEAS

EASTER CAKE

Cover a square cake with pale lemon royal icing. Place on square board. Make a pattern for the large letter E by tracing onto tracing or greaseproof paper. Scribe the E on the cake surface. Outline the letter with a dark yellow icing in a small bag fitted with a No1 tube, then flood with the same shade of runout icing.

Using a small cranked palette knife, smooth some green royal icing around the board. Place small mounds of sugarpaste on the sides of the cake, touching the board. Spread green royal icing over these, then gently pat the surface with a piece of foam rubber. Dust blue petal dust around the side to make the sky.

Pressure-pipe some rabbits on the side. With a No1 tube in a small bag filled with green royal icing, pipe grass and flower stems, leaves around the edge. Eject some small ejector blossoms on the sides.

When the E is dry, dust some blue around it and paint a small butterfly. Pipe some stems with a No1 tube. Using a small petal tube, pipe some daffodils directly onto the stems. Pipe in some leaves by cutting a V into the end of a bag. Spread some icing along the base of the E, then pipe the rest of the inscription with No1 tube and pipe a pressure-piped rabbit.

Pipe a shell edging around the top edge to finish the cake.

FLOWER BASKET CAKE

Coat the cake with pale yellow royal icing; finish with a bevelled edge. Pipe the basket as described on page 120 and fill with small flowers. With No46 tube pipe a bold heart shape shell, trying to pipe an equal number on each side. Pipe the bottom shell in the same way. Overpipe each shell with a C shape using a No2 tube and a darker colour. Pipe top border, then bottom. Pipe loops.

CORNELLI WORK CAKE

Cover the cake with coffee-coloured sugarpaste. Scribe the design onto the cake. With a No0 tube pipe cornelli work with cream-coloured royal icing. Pipe snailstrail around all edges except the flower. Outline the flower with a No1 tube. The centre of the flower is worked with pulled dots and then filled in with dark brown dots. Pipe a dark brown snailstrail all around the outer edge of the design. Work the design on the side of the cake similarly over the ribbon. Pipe a bottom border of cornelli work topped with a dark brown snailstrail. Pipe shells around the bottom edge of the cake. Overpipe each shell with brown S-shapes. Pipe a scratch line on the cake board around each shell.

LACE WEDDING CAKE

25 cm (10 in) and 18 cm (7 in) square rich fruit cakes,
marzipanned and royal iced on 30 cm (12 in) and 23 cm
(9 in) square silver cake boards
500 g (1 lb/3½ Cups) royal icing
3 metres (3 yds) 2.5 cm (1 in) white ribbon
3 metres (3 yds) 1 cm (½ in) fancy yellow ribbon
8 small and 8 medium-sized silver horseshoes
Sugar bell or flowers
Ribbons to decorate
4 white square cake pillars

Cut two squares of greaseproof or tracing paper to match the size of the top of each cake. Fold in half diagonally twice to make a triangle. Measure and mark triangles 5 cm (2 in) and 3.5 mm (1½ in) up from base (see below) and cut to make 2 templates. Place template on each cake and mark around cut shape with a pin.

Fit paper piping bags one with a No1 and a second bag with a No2 plain writing tube. Fill with royal icing and fold down tops. Using No2 tube, pipe over the design line on top of the cake from corner to corner with one continuous thread of icing to cover the marked lines. Repeat to pipe a second line of icing 1 cm (½ in) apart from first line. Pipe a line of icing along each top edge of cake. Using No1 piping tube, overpipe lines of icing with a fine icing line. Using No2 tube, pipe beads of icing a little apart between piped lines on top of the cake and at base and top edges on all sides of the cake. Using No1 tube, pipe cornelli work to fill in each triangle with a continuous thread of icing, on top of the cake board (for further details see page 113). Join up the beads of icing on the side of the cake with small threads of icing using a No1 plain writing tube. Repeat the same design on the remaining cake.

Measure and fit white ribbon around sides of both cakes, securing with a little icing. Repeat with yellow ribbon and tie 16 tiny bows and attach them to the sides and corners of the cakes, securing with a little icing. Place small horseshoes in position on the top and large base corners of the cakes using a little icing. Leave cake to dry in a warm, dry place.

To assemble, place the four pillars evenly spaced apart on the large cake, then place second cake in centre on top of pillars. Place sugar bell and ribbons or flower arrangement in centre on top of cake.

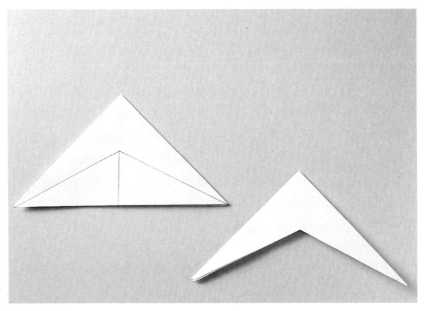

CHRISTENING CAKE

18 cm (7 in) square tier of Lace Wedding Cake
250 g (8 oz/1 ½ Cups) royal icing
Pink or blue food colouring
2 metres (2 yds) 2.5 cm (1 in) pink or blue ribbon
2 metres (2 yds) 5 mm (¼ in) pink or blue ribbon
1 Christening ornament (optional)

Remove the white and yellow ribbon from Lace Wedding Cake and detach the horseshoes. Colour royal icing pale pink or pale blue with food colouring, to match the ribbon. Fit a paper piping bag with a No1 plain writing tube. Fill with pink or blue icing and fold down top. Pipe beads of coloured icing over white beads of icing on the top, sides and base of the cake.

Tie and fit the ribbons around the outside of the cake and secure with icing. Tie fine ribbon into eight tiny bows and secure onto side and corners of cake with icing. Place ornament if desired.

LETTERING

So often it is necessary to write a message on the cake, but often even quite skilled cake decorators find this difficult to do well. Several different techniques are covered in this chapter and a variety of scripts and messages given for you to trace and copy

If lettering is not your forté then it is wise to either pipe on a plaque or pipe the inscriptions on waxed paper and transfer to the cake when completed – at least this way you can have more than one attempt at getting it right. The cakes here have been decorated with this in mind and using these techniques even a beginner could write the perfect inscription.

LETTERING TECHNIQUES

Lettering is one of the more problematic aspects of cake decorating, for poor lettering could spoil an otherwise excellent piece of work. Good lettering takes a great deal of practice to achieve.

An experienced decorator will be able to pipe lettering directly onto the cake freehand, but for most people it is best to draw a plan of the cake top and experiment to find the best style, size and position for the letters. The chosen lettering can then be traced and scratched onto the surface of the cake in the correct position before piping.

When piping letters, take care not to form bulbs of icing where lines begin or join. Neaten any ugly joins with a dampened paintbrush. If letters are still imperfect, overpipe the lines with very small dots or a fine snailstrail using a No0 or 00 tube.

When piping on a sugarpasted cake, be careful not to rest your hand on the edge of the cake, as this may spoil the surface. Instead, rest your forearm on a turntable slightly higher than the cake and positioned just to the side.

Piping directly onto the cake with a strong colour can be risky, as the colour will stain the surface, making it difficult to correct mistakes. A better method is to pipe the lettering first in icing to match the base-coat, then overpipe with coloured icing.

Lettering can also be done with runouts on waxed paper and then positioned on the cake with royal icing when dry. This is more suitable for doing numbers or initials than for greetings.

A series of greetings are given on pages 252 – 253.

This plaque shows various inscriptions, all piped directly onto the surface with a No1 or 0 tube.

1 *Place a small amount of icing in the bag and begin writing using firm but even pressure. Take care to get the spacing even and ensure that all the tops and tails are of equal height.*

2 *Words on the second line should be spaced centrally below the first line.*

133

RUNOUT LETTERING

This method is worked on waxed paper and then transferred to the cake when dry.

1 *Make the icing numeral using the template provided to outline the figures. Use white royal icing and a No1 tube. Allow to dry.*

2 *Paint the outline with silver food colouring, if desired.*

3 *Flood in the numbers with white or coloured runout icing. Allow to dry.*

4 *Numerals attached to cake top.*

GILDED LETTERS

The runout letters are made in white and when dry painted gold or silver. Gold and silver comes in powder and liquid form. The powder has to be mixed with clear alcohol (gin, vodka, etc.). Use the liquid in accordance with manufacturer's instructions.

When dry stick onto cake surface and gild with a small paintbrush. The other lettering styles are piped with white icing directly onto the plaque and gilded when completely dry.

MONOGRAMS

Monograms make a good decoration for a birthday cake or the initials of a couple intertwined are excellent on engagement and anniversary cakes.

Trace the two letters for the monogram on separate pieces of tracing or greaseproof (waxed) paper.

Move the letters about until you can overlap them with minimum crossovers. If too much of one letter is covered up, it is hard to read the finished monogram.

Once you are happy with the positioning, pin the papers together or place a piece of sticky tape over them to stop them moving.

Make a tracing of the completed monogram. Scribe onto the plaque or cake surface using a scriber or a hat pin. Outline with ordinary consistency icing using a No0 or 1 tube, depending on the letter size.

The partly completed monogram. The N has been flooded. Let dry for about 30 minutes, then flood the S. It is important to dry one letter first because if you flood both letters at the same time, they merge into each other and definition is lost. Monograms can be flooded in the same colours, different colours or shades of the same colour.

WRITING IN A CIRCLE

Writing in a circle looks good on a round cake. A posy or runout design could be placed in the centre of the circle. Pipe lettering before adding the centre decoration.

Place a round thin cake board on top of the cake. Make sure the board is large enough so that the centre decoration will fit. Decide on how much space the lettering will take up, then start piping. The tails of the Ps, Ys, and Gs are piped after the board is removed. Continue until the inscription is finished, remove the board and pipe any tails. Place the centre decoration in position.

COMMERCIAL SCRIPTS

This plaque shows a few of the many types of silver and gold plastic scripts and numerals available. These can be used on cakes or plaques. If you do not feel confident to write on a cake or are short of time these are an acceptable alternative.

EMBOSSED SCRIPTS

This plaque shows how to use plastic embossing script. Push the plastic piece into the paste covering of the cake or plaque within 15 minutes of coating, before a surface crust forms. Push into the paste in a straight movement – do not move about or you will get a distorted impression. Once pushed in, pull out straight to get a clean finish. When the impression is made you can leave it, or overpipe or outline the letters when the paste is dry.

DECORATING IDEAS

There are many ways to write 'Happy Christmas' but it is important to find a lettering style to complement the cake you are decorating. Here is a selection of Christmas cakes, note how the size and style of the writing is complementary to each of the cakes. These lettering techniques could be easily adapted to suit other occasions such as birthdays and anniversaries.

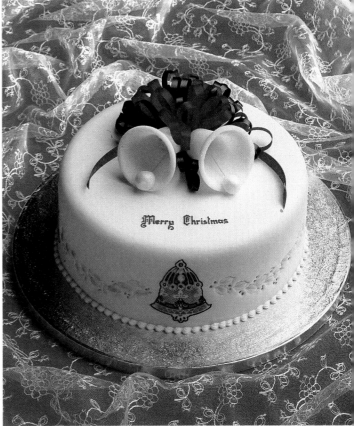

More examples of lettering styles for Christmas cakes; the fisrt is runout lettering made separately then attached to the cake, the second is freestyle piped directly onto cake.

40 CAKE

*25 cm (10 in) round fruit cake, marzipanned and royal iced
    in white on a 30 cm (12 in) silver drum board*
1 kg (2 lb/7 Cups) royal icing
Apricot food colouring

Using purchased door numbers as templates , place
on cake top and draw outline. Then, using a No2
tube and white icing pipe the outline of the numbers.
Colour one-third of the icing apricot and flood in
outlines and leave to dry. Pipe small flowers on the
numbers using a No1 tube and white icing.

To work the lettering write the greeting in bold
script on a piece of card, then separate the letters
into groups for easy piping (see page 252 for script).
Cover the script with waxed paper and pipe the
greeting in white using a No3 tube; leave to dry.
Overpipe the script with apricot icing using the No2
tube and leave to dry. Carefully peel off the paper
and fix with icing to the cake.

Pipe white bulbs on the top and bottom edges
using a No3 tube and white icing. Link the bulbs
in white with a No3 tube and overpipe in apricot
with a No2 tube. Pipe flowers on centre of sides with
No1 tube in apricot.

Detail of cake side decoration.

Purchased door numbers.

Writing the script, piping in white and overpiping in apricot.

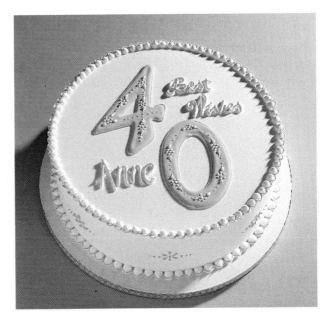

HAPPY BIRTHDAY

25 cm (10 in) round fruit cake, marzipanned and royal icing
  in cream on a 30 cm (12 in) cake board
750 g (1½ lb/5¼ Cups) royal icing
Cream and brown food colouring
2 metres (2 yds) narrow white ribbon
Purchased decoration

Draw parallel lines 8 cm (3½ in) apart on top of the cake. With a No2 tube and white icing, continue to pipe the line around margin of the cake as shown following the drawn line. Pipe a second line inside the first, this time with a No1 tube. Inside this line pipe a further line of dots.

To make the letters, trace the larger outline letters onto card (page 252), then fix waxed paper on top.

Using a No2 tube and thinned white icing fill in the outlined shape of the letters; leave to dry. Colour a small amount of icing to rich creamy coffee colour and overpipe the letters using a No2 tube. Leave until completely dry. Carefully peel the letters off the waxed paper and fix in position in the centre of the cake securing with dabs of white icing.

Using a No44 tube pipe a shell border around the bottom edge angling the piping so that the thickest part of the shell is nearest to the cake, tapering to the outside edge of the board, as in the photograph. The dots are then piped with a No1 tube in the dark cream icing.

Fix two rows of narrow ribbon around the sides and place the purchased decoration on top.

The traced letters are covered with waxed paper, filled in with white icing and then overpiped in dark cream.

CONGRATULATIONS CAKE

25 cm (10 in) square fruit cake, marzipanned and royal iced
   in white on a 30 cm (12 in) cake board
1 kg (2 lb/7 Cups) royal icing
Navy blue food colouring
1½ metre (1½ yd) 1 cm (½ in) blue ribbon
Silk flowers
60 – 90 g (2 – 3 oz) sugarpaste

Take a piece of white sugarpaste and roll into a long strip 25 x 2 cm (10 x ¾ in) wide. Cut the left-hand end into a V-shape. With a No2 tube and white icing pipe C O N G R A T U L A T I O N S. Fold the end of the strip as shown and trim off excess, then cut a V-shape in the second end. Prop up the folds and leave to dry for several days until hard.

Colour about one-quarter of the icing blue and use to overpipe the letters with a No1 tube. Pipe a thin blue shell edging round the edge of the scroll and leave to dry.

Place the scroll on the cake just below the centre, then, using a No2 tube, pipe three lines in white just below the scroll. Overpipe in blue using the No1 tube. Pipe a shell edge using a No44 tube in white icing around the top, then pipe blue dots between the shells. Pipe tassel shells with No44 tube and white icing around the bottom edge. Link alternate shells with a No2 tube and white icing. Overpipe with the No1 tube in blue, place dots at the top of each to finish.

Fix the ribbon around the sides of the cake and add the silk flowers.

Making the sugarpaste scroll, piping the letters and overpiping in blue.

141

FRILLS AND FLOUNCES

Frills and flounces look wonderful on sugarpasted cakes and are really impressive. The basic frill, however, is only made with a pastry cutter and a cocktail stick (toothpick) and is not at all difficult. It is necessary to strengthen the sugarpaste to make these frills but this is easy and instructions are given in the chapter.

The anniversary cakes illustrate how lovely frills look on the finished cake. The frills on the silver anniversary cake are dusted with shimmering petal dust which catches the light and looks so pretty while the golden anniversary cake leaves the frills plain but uses the same basic technique to make the little carnations.

FRILLS AND FLOUNCES

Frills and flounces are a delicate finishing touch on a cake. The frill is the invention of Elaine Garrett, a South African cake decorator.

Special round or straight cutters with scalloped edges are used to create the frill.

Knead 5 ml (1 teaspoon) gum tragacanth into 500 g (1 lb) sugarpaste and leave for at least 24 hours. This will enable the frill to keep its lift without drooping when placed on the cake.

Frills are easier to attach to a firm surface, so allow the sugarpaste on the cake to dry for a few days.

If a crimped edge is desired the frill must, however, be applied when the paste on the cake is soft. This crimping can disguise a poor edge.

Before applying the frill pipe a snailstrail around the base of the cake. It is important that this edge is finished off neatly as it will be visible at the points where the frill lifts.

Roll the paste thinly and cut out a circle with a scalloped cutter. Remove a centre circle of paste. The size of this removed circle determines the width of the frill. Cut out a large inside circle for a narrow frill and a small inside circle for a deeper one.

Cut the frill and open up the circle until fairly straight. Be careful with the middle area of the upper edge as this is the weakest point.

Scribe a line onto the cake where the frill is to be attached. Place the frill near the edge of the board. Lay a cocktail stick (toothpick) halfway up the paste and, putting an index finger on top of the stick, rotate it. As the stick moves forward over the paste it will make the frill. Repeat along the entire edge of the paste.

Moisten the cake below the scribed line with a little water and attach the frill. Smooth over the upper edge gently with your thumb. Raise the frill with the end of a paintbrush to give lift where needed. When adding the second frill, butt the edges together and turn under the extreme edge of the frill so that it appears to form a natural fold.

Several methods can be used to finish off the upper edge of the frill. Try piping a snailstrail, cross-stitch or dots. Small lace sections can look very attractive. Plunger cutter flowers also produce a pleasing effect.

For a more definite lift use a flouncing or anger tool rotated gently in the same manner on the edge of the paste.

The cake's colour scheme can be emphasized by graduating the shade of each layer of frills, starting with the darkest shade for the lowest layer. Petal dusting powder can also be applied to the edge of the frill.

PLAIN FRILL

1 *Roll out some paste, and cut out using a plain pastry cutter.*

2 *Cut the circle in half.*

3 *Frill each half, carefully using a cocktail stick (toothpick).*

4 *Lay one half on top of the other, sticking together with a little egg white.*

5 *Cut out centre of semi-circle, adjusting width of frill. When dry, dust the edge with petal dust.*

Opposite: White wedding cake, for detail of lace work see page 249.

GARRETT FRILL

1 *Cut-out paste.*

2 *Starting to frill.*

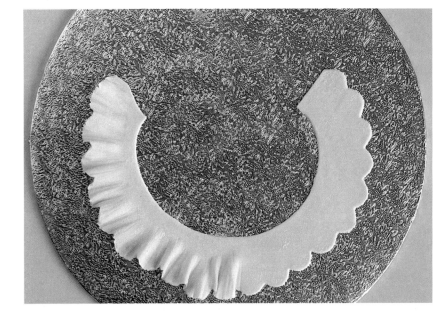

3 *Frill ready for attaching.*

FRILLED PLAQUES

A little plaque made from a Garrett frill cutter would be suitable for any type of cake. A small runout, painting or spray of flowers could be put on the plaque with an inscription. If you feel unhappy about writing straight onto the cake surface writing on a plaque is safer, if you do make a mistake you can always make another plaque, but a drastic mistake on a cake can result in having to take off all the icing and re-coating it.

Cut out the plaque with a pastry cutter and frill the edge of the circle. For a double frill cut a second plaque with a smaller cutter, brush a little egg white into the centre of the larger plaque and attach the smaller one on top. Using the thicker end of the pastry cutter mark a ring as a piping guide. Dry for 2–3 hours.

To decorate, brush the outer edge of the frill with a little petal dust and paint a design in the centre. For the double plaque, pipe a small shell around the marked circle and write a message. The sample here is finished with a ribbon bow.

147

ATTACHING THE FRILL

1 *Make a paper template to indicate the curve of the frill, attach to the cake securely with pins.*

2 *Using a scriber or needle scribe the curve-line on the cake.*

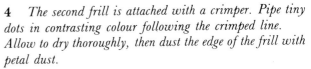

3 *Attach the frill to the cake using a little egg-white or water.*

4 *The second frill is attached with a crimper. Pipe tiny dots in contrasting colour following the crimped line. Allow to dry thoroughly, then dust the edge of the frill with petal dust.*

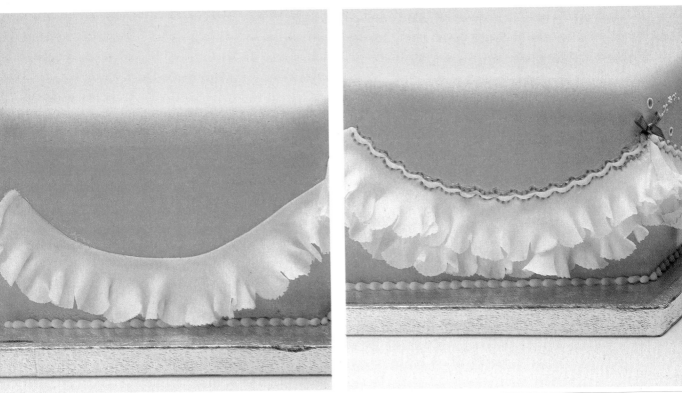

DECORATIVE FRILLS

1 *Single frill with bows.*

2 *Scalloped frill.*

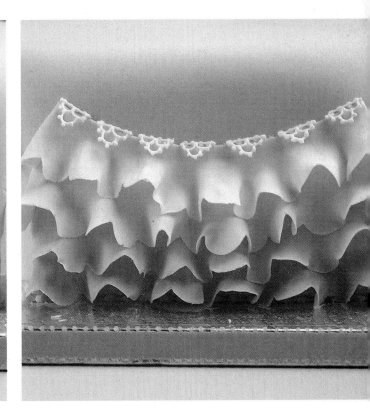

3 *Double frill with appliquéd heart motif.*

4 *Tiered coloured frills.*

STRAIGHT FRILLS

This plaque shows straight frills as an alternative to scalloped frills.

1 *This shows a double frill. The top layer is embossed with a daisy and leaf design. When dry, dust the bottom edge. Pearls have been placed on the top edge.*

2 *The frill shown here has forget-me-nots and leaves painted with food colouring. Once dry, dust the edge.*

3 *Another double-layered frill with embossed daisies along its length. Paint in the stems and centres of the daisies.*

4 *This narrow double frill has tiny piped dots all over the surface.*

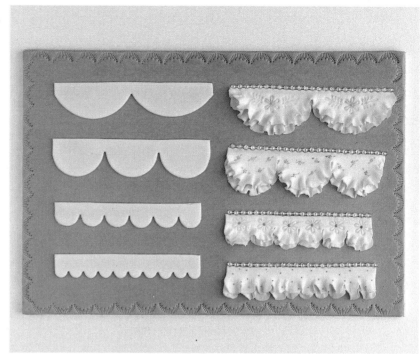

FRILLED LEAVES

Colour some sugarpaste green. Roll out thinly on a lightly cornfloured (cornstarched) surface. Using a cocktail cutter or a cardboard template, cut out the leaf shape. Using a cocktail stick (toothpick) start frilling the edge. Continue frilling all the way around the edge of the leaf. Place on a piece of foam rubber. Mark the veins on the leaf with a sharp knife.

To finish off the leaf mark the central vein and leave to dry. The leaves can be placed over formers or crumpled up tissues so they dry in natural, individual form.

PASTRY CUTTER CARNATION

These quick little carnations are made with sugarpaste. They can be made in white and dusted with petal dust or, as shown, in a pastel shade and then dusted with additional petal dust to give a natural effect.

The carnation sizes can be altered by using different sized cutters: the smaller the cutter, the smaller the finished flower will be. In damp humid conditions a little gum tragacanth should be kneaded into the paste. Use approximately 2.5 ml (½ teaspoon) to 250 g (8 oz) of paste. Leave 30 minutes before using. Keep in a polythene bag to prevent it from drying out.

1 *Roll out the paste thinly on a lightly cornfloured (cornstarched) surface and, using a serrated pastry cutter, cut out the shape. Cut a hole in the centre using a small round cutter then with a cocktail stick (toothpick) dipped in a little cornflour (cornstarch), frill the edges all the way around, then cut open the ring with a sharp knife.*

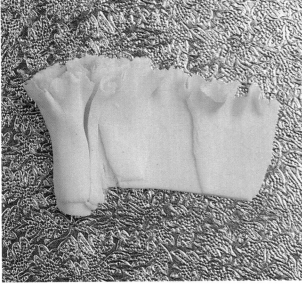

2 *Gently use your fingers to pleat the straight side and shape into a straight edge. Do not worry if the bottom cracks, as it will be trimmed off afterwards. Brush some egg white along the strip from the bottom to where the frill starts. Starting at the left-hand end, roll up. The first 5 cm (2 in) should be rolled tightly to ensure a good centre and overall shape.*

3 *Continue rolling, making sure the overlap is stuck round, then use scissors to cut off the excess paste. Leave to dry.*

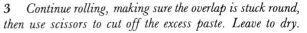

THE DRAPE

A drape can be used in conjunction with the Garrett frill or on its own on a plain cake. Knead 5 ml (1 teaspoon) gum tragacanth into 500 g (1 lb) sugarpaste and leave for at least 24 hours.

Make a paper template larger than the cake board. The drape on the cake illustrated is 33 cm (13 in) in diameter; the cake board is 28 cm (11 in). Measure out six points on the edge of the template. Mark the six points on the cake.

1 *Roll out the sugarpaste on cornflour (cornstarch) until it is almost transparent.*

2 *Place the template on the paste and cut around it with a tracing wheel to make an attractive edge.*

3 *To attach the drape it is not necessary to moisten either cake or paste. Match up the six marks. Lift the side of the drape and secure with a cocktail stick (toothpick) at each of the six marks. When dry remove the sticks by twisting before pulling out.*

DECORATING IDEAS

WEDDING BELL
Bake two cakes in a bell-shaped tin (pan) or in pudding basins, cover with marzipan and sugarpaste. Allow to dry for at least 48 hours, then make and attach the Garrett frills as instructed in this chapter. Decorate the upper edge of the frill with a piped embroidery design as shown or with any of the other finishes illustrated in chapter 9. Attach two drooping flower arrangements to the bells and finish the board with a ribbon trim.

CAKE WITH DRAPE
Cover a 20 cm (8 in) cake with marzipan and with white sugarpaste in the normal way. Roll out the sugarpaste for the drape, cut out and attach following the instruction on facing page. Finish the drape by piping small dots of icing on the drape using a No0 or No1 tube. Pipe dots on the bottom cut edge of the drape to neaten. Pipe around the base of the cake as shown.

Attach three small sugar or silk flower and ribbon bouquets at alternate points on the drape and a single flower with a ribbon loop at the remaining points. Trim the board with matching ribbon.

AMERICAN-STYLE WEDDING CAKE
Cover both tiers with pale lemon sugarpaste. Place the top tier on a piece of card the same size as the base and attach to the bottom tier with a small piece of sugarpaste. Pipe a snailstrail around the base of the cake and where the two tiers join. Attach the frills and decorate with miniature green bows.

The large wired spray is made with daisies, ivy and pulled blossom. Stick into a posy pick inserted in the top of the cake. Once the spray is in position, put some pale lemon sugarpaste over the base and smooth over with a palette knife to cover both the pick and the hole. Finish off the cake with piped doves and green velvet ribbon.

SILVER WEDDING CAKE

20 cm (8 in) oval rich or light fruit cake, marzipanned
25 cm (10 in) oval silver cake board
1 kg (2 lb) sugarpaste
250 g (8 oz) strengthened sugarpaste (see page 145)
Violet food colouring
Icing (confectioner's) sugar to dust
1 egg white
1 metre (1 yd) 2.5 cm (1 in) fancy silver ribbon
'25' silver emblem
2 silver double bell emblems
Silver petal dust

Tint sugarpaste and strengthened paste pale mauve with food colouring. Roll out sugarpaste thinly on surface dusted with icing (confectioner's) sugar and cover cake. Smooth and trim sugarpaste to fit.

Measure and fit ribbon around outside of cake, secure at the back of the cake with a stainless steel pin. Tie a separate bow and secure at front of cake with a pin. Cut remaining ribbon into two thin strips and tie two small bows.

Roll out one small piece of strengthened paste into a long thin strip and trim to 1 cm (½ in) wide. Frill paste using a cocktail stick (toothpick), place on cake board and attach to the base of cake, using a little egg white to secure. Repeat to make enough paste frills to go around the cake board. Make a second frill to go over first frill, trim to fit. Repeat this double

frill edging around the top edge of cake. Roll out a piece of strengthened paste thinly, cut out a 5 cm (2 in) oval using a cutter. Frill the edge and place the '25' emblem in centre, arrange in centre of cake. Secure two double bells and small bows at opposite sides on top of cake, using a small piece of petal paste. Dust frills with silver petal dust using a fine paintbrush. Leave in a warm place to dry.

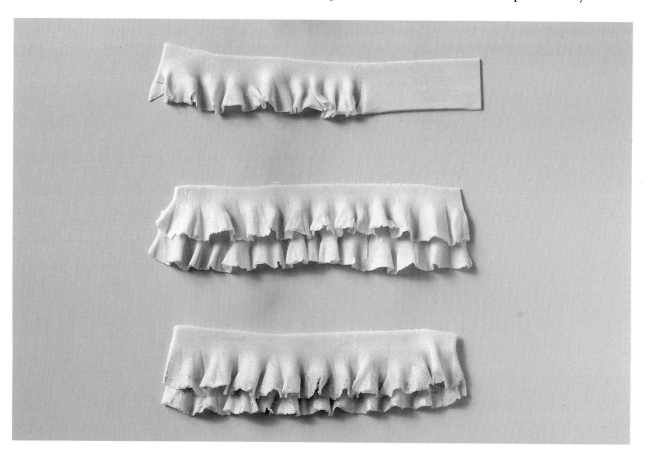

154

GOLDEN WEDDING CAKE

25 x 20 cm (10 x 8 in) rich or light fruit cake, marzipanned
30 x 25 cm (12 x 10 in) silver or gold cake board
1.5 kg (2½ lb) sugarpaste
Icing (confectioner's) sugar to dust
Golden yellow food colouring
1½ metres (1½ yds) 2.5 cm (1 in) fancy gold ribbon
250 g (8 oz) strengthened sugarpaste (see page 145)
10 white Garrett frills
1 egg white
9 sugarpaste carnations and 1 bud
4 gold horseshoes
Gold petal dust
10 gold paper leaves
1 gold double bell
1 gold 'Happy Anniversary' emblem

Colour sugarpaste golden yellow with food colouring. Roll out thinly and cover cake, smooth and trim the sugarpaste. Crimp top edge of sugarpaste using a crimping tool. Measure and fit ribbon around side of cake, securing with a stainless steel pin. Cut remaining ribbon into thin strips and tie four small bows.

Use strengthened paste to make Garrett frills. Make one frill at a time and cut in half, attach to one corner of the cake 2.5 cm (1 in) up from the cake board and secure with egg white. Secure second frill just above first, to overlap. Repeat to attach five frilled layers in each corner. Make carnations, sprinkle with petal dust and arrange two at each corner with a bow, horseshoe and two gold leaves. Press the bells in position on front side of cake and position 'Happy Anniversary' emblem, remaining carnation bud and gold leaves in centre of cake. Leave in a warm, dry place until the sugarpaste has hardened.

1 *Crimping top edge of cake.*

2 *Showing overlapping Garrett frills.*

3 *Making sugarpaste carnations.*

SUGARPASTE TECHNIQUES

Sugarpaste lends itself to a wide variety of decorative styles. Embossing and crimping are two such techniques which add decorative touches with relatively little effort. Similarly with ribbon insertion and banding. The effect is superb, but the skill easy to master. The technique of appliqué is taken from needlework and works well in sugarpaste and following on from this is the more complicated bas relief work which does require some experience to do well.

The cakes shown here demonstrate how well sugarpaste works with strong colours. The All Hallows cake uses appliqué skills while the chocolate box demonstrates the use of crimping and the elegant two-tier cake uses ribbon insertion to great effect.

CRIMPER WORK

Crimper tools, sometimes called nippers, come in a combination of different shapes and widths. The most commonly used ones are 10 mm (⅜ in) wide and come in nine shapes: straight, curve, oval, V, diamond, scallop, double scallop, heart and holly (see page 12 for further details).

The shapes can be used on their own or combined to make a great number of different patterns. Crimper work can also be used attractively with other techniques, such as embroidery, lace, ribbon work, with embossing, appliqué, over-piping, or for disguising the join of the flounce to the cake.

Practise the design on a piece of sugarpaste before coating the cake.

Crimper work must be done on freshly applied sugarpaste. The crimpers must be clean and dry. Dust them with a little cornflour (cornstarch) to prevent sticking. Adjust the crimpers to the right aperture, which depends on the size of the design, and hold with an elastic band. The wider the aperture, the more ridged effect will result when the crimpers are closed. Adjust the aperture by sliding the elastic band higher or lower along the crimper.

To make a crimper design, insert the crimpers into the sugarpaste, pinch together, release and move. If you forget to release the crimpers, a section of the paste will be torn.

If combining crimper work with ribbon banding, use a pair of dividers to mark both the line where the ribbon will be fastened and the lines where the crimper work will go. Complete the crimper work before adding the ribbon and the embroidery.

Embroidery between the two bands of curves gives a very dainty effect. A slight variation is the use of embroidery and embossing in alternate ovals. Combinations of appliqué and embroidery can also give a variety of effects.

On wedding or engagement cakes, very pretty designs can be created with the heart-shaped crimpers. The design can be emphasized with embroidery or embossing. Butterflies can be created by using the heart-shaped crimpers in pairs, with a body piped between.

If there is a scalloped design on the side of a cake which will be decorated with lace, it makes an attractive change to mark out the scallops using a variety of crimpers. Once the coating has set, apply the lace as usual.

The Garrett frill or the flounce is usually attached when the coating has set. The join then has to be finished off with embroidery, snailstrail or stitching, but it will always be obvious how the frill or flounce

was done. If, however, the flounce or frill is attached to the cake while the icing is still fresh, it is possible to completely disguise how it was attached by using crimper work on the join. Be careful not to cut through the frill. Most of the crimping is done on the cake rather than on the frill.

Crimping can be used as a border around the base of a cake, especially by beginners who might lack confidence to pipe a border with royal icing. Simply roll out a thin sausage of paste, long enough to go around the cake. Cut the sausage ends at an angle, place round the cake and butt the ends together. Then crimp the border.

EMBOSSING

Embossing is similar to crimper work, as it also must be done while the sugarpaste is fresh. The two techniques can be used in conjunction with each other.

Many different tools can be used to impress a pattern into the paste. Leather embossing tools, which are available in many different patterns, are very effective. Decorative spoon handles can produce interesting effects. To add delicate finishing touches to small scallops and flowers, try using the tops of icing tubes.

Embossing can be used on the cake board as well as the cake. It also looks effective as an edging around a plaque.

Both crimper work and embossing can be used effectively with other techniques such as embroidery and ribbon insertion. Colour can be added by picking out areas with dusting powder or painting with food colouring.

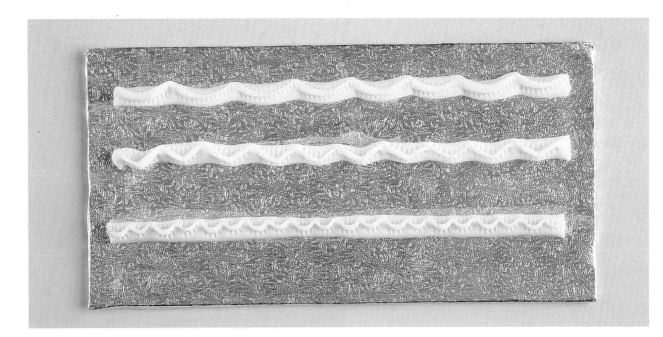

1 *Crimped edging.*

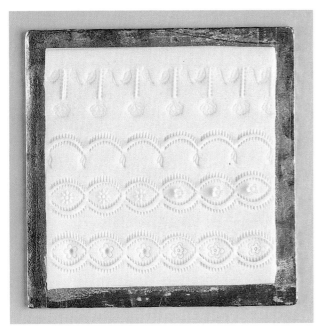

2 *Sample crimping using crimpers in combination with embossing tools.*

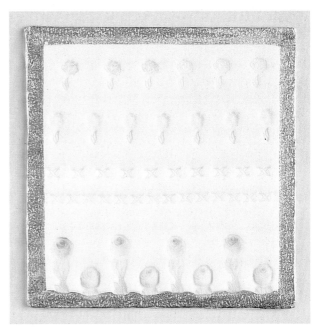

3 *Plain and tinted embossing.*

RIBBON INSERTION

This technique creates the illusion that ribbon has been threaded through the sugarpaste. The width of the ribbon can range from very fine to about 1 cm (½ in). For an elegant effect choose colours to match the sugarpaste and embroidery. Contrasting colours will result in a brighter look.

The section where the ribbon is to be placed should be measured first and marked with either a pin or a scriber so that the lines are straight and the ribbon lengths will be separated by equal spaces of icing.

Insert the ribbon while the sugarpaste is still soft. Make a slit in the paste using a scalpel or ribbon inserting tool. Take care that the slit is not so deep that it reaches the marzipan beneath the sugarpaste (see left).

For narrow ribbon inserts, fold a piece of ribbon about 1 cm (½ in) long in half and place in the slit with tweezers.

For wider ribbon inserts cut the ribbon slightly longer than the space between the slits. The ribbon should be long enough so that it makes a loop and does not lie flat on the cake. Each loop should be the same distance away from the cake. Experiment with the first piece of ribbon and when satisfied, carefully remove it so as not to damage slits and cut all the pieces to this length.

Moisten each cut edge of ribbon with a little egg white and use tweezers to place one edge in each slit.

Ribbon insertion looks effective with other techniques such as crimping, broderie anglaise and lacework. Lace pieces can be applied between the loops of ribbon or attached to the edge or edges of flat ribbon banding. Embroidery can be piped onto the ribbon, or onto the cake to give the appearance of holding the ribbon in place.

RIBBON BANDING

Banding is a way of using ribbon to finish off a cake and bring out one or two of its colours. Ribbons in different shades of the same colour make a lovely subtle effect.

The bands of ribbon should be applied when the sugarpaste is dry. Pipe dots of icing onto the cake and place the ribbon on top immediately. Hide the join where the two ends overlap with a small neat bow in the same colour.

Stagger the bows so that they are not one above the other as this would make the cake look cluttered (see below).

APPLIQUÉ

The technique of appliqué consists of applying cutout shapes of material to the surface of other material, one shape can be laid on top of another to build up the picture.

APPLIQUÉ LION

1 *Body stuck to base. Legs moistened and laid in position on top.*

2 *Add mane and ears. Continue to add the eyes, nose and muzzle to build up the lion.*

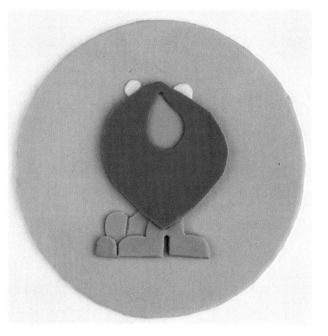

3 *Add black eyebrows, black nose and pupils of the eyes.*

4 *Paint black detail.*

SPRAY FLOWERS

Trace the template and scribe the pattern onto a cake or plaque. Paint in stems using a No0 paintbrush. Use green to paint in the small leaves. Trace the pattern for the large leaves and petals onto paper or card and cut out. Roll out paste of the desired colours. Cut out petals and leaves. Stick onto surface with egg white, then dry. Start with the flower furthest away from you, for example the pink blossom on the right is slightly under the large rose so attach the blossom first.

BAS RELIEF

Bas relief is a technique which will produce a shallow relief or two-dimensional design on the surface of a cake or plaque. It can be straightforward or complicated, depending on the design chosen. Until proficient in this technique it is preferable to work on a plaque so that mistakes can be more easily corrected. This will have an added benefit as this technique is quite time-consuming in that the plaque can be kept as a memento long after the cake has been eaten.

The principle is similar to a runout where the picture is created by completing the background first, then working gradually forward.

For bas relief a combination of sugarpaste and modelling paste is used.

The sugarpaste is used principally for building up the main body of the design. The modelling paste (see page 66) is more pliable and is used to drape, cover or clothe the shapes or figures. As both pastes are quite soft, a modelling tool can be used to form depressions, creases and curves.

The main object is to mould and attach the clothing or covering in such a way that it appears to encircle the figure or shape, giving a three-dimensional effect.

For finishing details a number of techniques are used. Add the features and any patterning or shading on clothing with dusting colour and liquid food colouring. Pipe in the hair. Paint the immediate foreground, add flowers and grasses using the modelling paste.

This plaque has been decorated with an appliqué flower design. Roll out the coloured paste so it is translucent, cut out using a modelling knife.

TEDDY BEAR QUILT

Cut out the background shapes first: the bed and the bear's head and feet.

The inside of the pillow is modelled, allowed to dry, then painted with stripes before it is wrapped with the outer pillow-case.

Roughly shape some paste to represent the bulk of the teddy's body under the bedclothes. Drape the quilt over and tuck the edges well down to give a natural rounded look. Add wash set, honey pot and slippers.

Divide the quilt into squares and paint every other square. When dry paint the rest. Allow to dry. Paint on the surface pattern using a No000 brush. The wash jug and basin are painted in the same way.

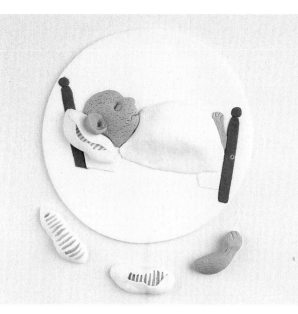

DECORATING IDEAS

HEART CAKE

Bake a sponge-type cake in a heart-shaped tin (pan) and cover with creamy-yellow sugarpaste. Emboss the top edge of the cake and down the point using a No2 crimper. Pipe an embroidered design using the picture as a guide using a No0 or No1 piping tube and creamy yellow royal icing. Make or purchase an orchid or other suitably coloured bouquet.

18TH BIRTHDAY CAKE

Make cakes in numeral tins (pans) or cut from 20 cm (8 in) squares, a 18 cm (7 in) round and a 15 cm (6 in) round tin (pan), cut the central holes with a pastry cutter. Cover with marzipan if fruit cakes are used or brush sponges with apricot glaze. Cut out a piece of sugarpaste the same size as the board and brush with a little water and attach. Use a No4 crimper to make parallel lines round board. Cover the cakes in sugarpaste and within 30 minutes use a No24 crimper to form textured pattern at base of cake. Use a No4 crimper to make the parallel lines of crimping allowing room for the ribbon to be attached on both the sides and top of cake. Position cakes on board. Pipe a dot of icing on ribbon end and place between parallel lines of crimping at back of cake, then pin in position. Proceed around the cake piping a small dot of icing every 7.5 cm (3 in)

and pinning in place. Allow to dry, then remove pins. Use a No42 piping tube to pipe shell border, then with yellow royal icing and a No2 tube pipe the thicker lines on top of the cake and then pipe thinner lines with No1 tube. Pipe inscription.

HEXAGONAL WEDDING CAKE

Work on one cake at a time to prevent sugarpaste from becoming too dry to crimp. Mark the limits of the area to be embossed by pressing a card template gently to the surface, then crimp along line with a No23 crimper. Use a cake decorator's or craft embossing tool to emboss the pattern beneath the crimped lines. Take care to emboss to same depth and at same angle. Dust with cornflour (cornstarch) if embosser begins to stick. Repeat for other cakes and leave for 24 hours. Make hexagonal plaque and crimp edges and attach to top tier for figures to stand on. Attach silk flowers and leaves and the ribbon banding with dabs of royal icing. Arrange cakes as shown and support top tier with four pillars and wooden skewers. Make sprays from silk flowers and make arching columns of flowers using florist's wire. Arrange on cakes with bride and groom figures.

SOPHISTICAKE

25 cm (10 in) and 20 cm (8 in) round sponge cakes
Apricot jam (jelly)
Buttercream icing made with 185 g (6 oz/¾ Cup) butter
  and 375 g (12 oz/1 ¾ Cups) icing (confectioner's) sugar
  (see page 54)
1.25 kg (2 ½ lb) sugarpaste
Heather food colouring
2 metres (2 yds) patterned ribbon
500 g (1 lb/3 ½ Cups) royal icing
Luxury chocolates

Cut the sponges in half and spread with jam (jelly). Put the large cake on a board. Spread a little buttercream on top. Place the small cake on the large one. Spread the buttercream over whole cake.

Colour the sugarpaste pale heather pink. Roll out thickly and use to cover cake, smooth and trim. Leave for a few hours until the sugarpaste has firmed slightly but is still soft. Make slits in the paste using a scalpel or ribbon inserting tool. Take care that the slit is not so deep that it reaches the buttercream. Cut the ribbon into equal pieces and using tweezers or a pointed knife, place one edge in each slit (see right). Make bows with remaining ribbon and attach to cake with a little royal icing.

Colour the royal icing dark heather pink and pipe round base of each cake. Decorate top with luxury chocolates.

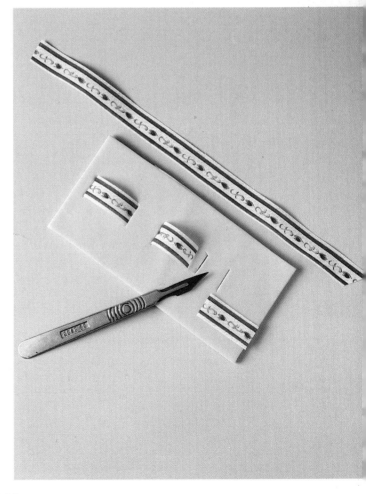

DAD'S CHOCOLATE BOX

3-egg quantity chocolate sponge mix baked in a 15 cm (6 in)
  square cake tin (pan)
Chocolate buttercream icing (made with 125 g (4 oz/½ Cup)
  butter, 250 g (8 oz/1½ Cups) icing (confectioner's) sugar
  (see page 54)
750 g (1½ lb) sugarpaste
Brown and black food colouring
1 metre (1 yard) ribbon

Cut the cake in half and spread with a little chocolate buttercream. Place the other half on top. Level top, put on board. Spread remaining icing over cake. Colour the sugarpaste a chocolate brown colour. Reserving 125 g (4 oz) roll out the sugarpaste and use to cover the cake. Smooth and trim. Using a ruler, mark a line 1 cm (½ in) down from the top, all around to represent the edge of the lid. Using a double scallop crimper, crimp around the top edge of the 'lid'. Using a straight and a curved crimper, mark a design on sides and top as illustrated. Roll out the remaining sugarpaste and, using an oval fluted cutter, cut out a plaque. Using alphabet cutters, cut out the initials of the recipient. Using a small fluted cutter, cut out a key hole surround. Using a little water, attach the plaque to the centre of the lid. Stick the letters on top and prick with a skewer. Attach the keyhole plate to front of cake, paint keyhole in black. Add ribbon.

Piece of icing showing crimping. Close-up on initials.

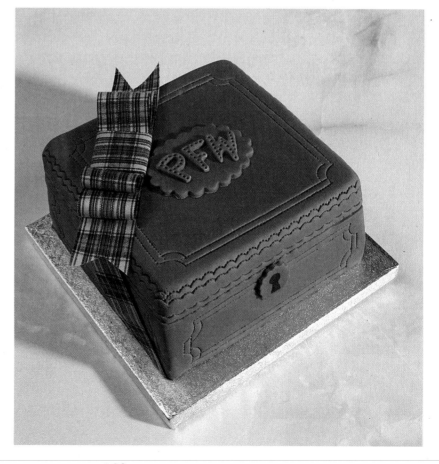

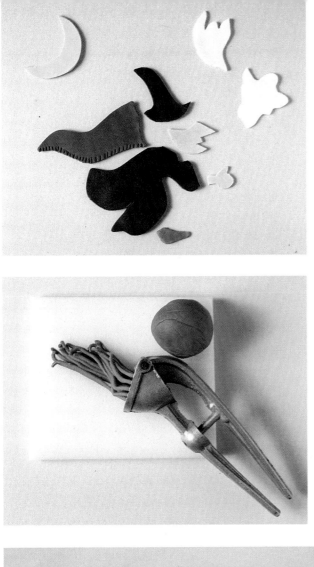

ALL HALLOWS CAKE

23 cm (9 in) round fruit cake, marzipanned
1.5 kg (3 lbs) sugarpaste
1 egg white, beaten
500 g (1 lb/3 ½ Cups) royal icing
Blue, yellow, purple, black, flesh and brown food colouring

Place the cake on a board. Colour two-thirds of the sugarpaste dark blue. Roll out. Brush cake with egg white and cover cake with sugarpaste. Of the remaining sugarpaste, roll out about one-third and, using the templates (page 250), cut out 9–10 ghosts. Attach to the side of the cake using egg white. Knead the trimmings into the remaining sugarpaste. Divide the sugarpaste into appropriate amounts for the witch and colour accordingly. Roll out and, using the templates, cut out the parts of the witch. Cut out a moon and, using a small cutter, the stars. For the broom-stick, roll three sausage-shaped pieces. For the hair and the broom, push brown sugarpaste through a garlic press. Attach all pieces to the cake using egg white. Place hat on witch's head after applying hair. Make two tiny balls of flesh-coloured sugarpaste and attach to face to resemble warts. Colour the royal icing dark blue. Using a piping bag fitted with a small writing tube, pipe eye on witch and eyes and mouths on ghosts. Put remaining royal icing in a piping bag fitted with a small star tube and pipe around base and top edge of cake.

1 *Pieces of witch and ghosts cut out of sugarpaste.*

2 *Make hair and broom using a garlic press.*

169

SUGARPASTE FLOWERS

Although it is possible to buy flowers for cake decoration, a better colour match and a wider range of flowers can be made from scratch, particularly on a wedding cake where it is nice to have the flowers to match the bride's bouquet. The flowers can be made using a variety of techniques, some using cutters and others requiring no special equipment at all. Many of the flowers are easier to make than they at first appear although they are delicate and patience and practice is required to make and colour them well.

The wedding cake with purple flowers is simply sugarpasted and decorated with sugarpaste roses and sprays of blossom. The 21st birthday cake is made from simple cutter flowers and blossom sprays.

FLOWER PASTE

All the moulded flowers in this book have been made using this recipe for flower paste. However, there are many variations on this recipe, so experiment to find one which suits you. Remember that flower paste is affected by climate, and if you live in a very humid place, then you need to add more cornflour (cornstarch) and reduce the amount of icing (confectioner's) sugar.

440 g (14 oz/2 ½ Cups) icing (confectioner's) sugar, sifted
60 g (2 oz/½ Cup) cornflour (cornstarch)
15 ml (3 teaspoons) gum tagacanth
25 ml (5 teaspoons) cold water
10 ml (2 teaspoons) powdered gelatine
15 ml (3 teaspoons) white fat (shortening)
10 ml (2 teaspoons) liquid glucose
1 large egg white, string removed

Sift together sugar and cornflour (cornstarch) in the bowl of a heavy duty mixer. Sprinkle over gum tragacanth. Place mixer bowl over a large pan of boiling water. Cover the top with a dry cloth, and then with a plate or cake board.

Put water in a small glass bowl and sprinkle powdered gelatine over it. Leave to sponge.

Half-fill a small saucepan with water and place over a low heat. Bring to just below the boiling point. Place bowl of sponged gelatine over pan and stir in liquid glucose and white fat. Stir until fat is melted.

When icing sugar feels warm, take bowl off pan of boiling water, dry the bottom and place on mixer. Add the gelatine solution and egg white to sugar. Cover bowl with a cloth, and turn mixer to the slowest speed. Mix until all the ingredients are combined and the paste is a dull beige colour.

Turn mixer to maximum and beat until paste is white and stringy. This will take 5–10 minutes. Remove paste from bowl and place in a clean plastic bag. Place bag in an airtight container and refrigerate for at least 24 hours before using. If planning to store paste for a few weeks, put it in four or five small bags and open one at a time.

To use paste, cut off a small piece, add a smear of white fat and dip into some egg white before working. The warmth of your hands will bring paste to a workable, elastic consistency. Remember that the paste dries out very quickly, so keep it covered at all times and never cut off more than a very small piece. Certain colours, particularly reds and violets, may change the consistency, so it may be necessary to add more white fat and egg white.

QUICK FLOWER PASTE

This paste is easier to make, but the flowers will not be as delicate.

250 g (8 oz) commercial sugarpaste
5 ml (1 teaspoon) gum tragacanth
White fat (shortening)

Knead the sugarpaste and gum tragacanth together, adding a small amount of white fat to get an elastic consistency. Store and use as for the previous recipe.

HINTS AND TIPS

Flower paste and modelling paste are affected by the warmth of your hands. A cake decorator with very warm hands would need to use a slightly firmer paste than someone with cold hands.

Always colour with paste food colourings, not liquid ones, which will change the consistency of the modelling paste. Add the colouring using the end of a cocktail stick (toothpick).

After colouring flower paste or sugarpaste, put it in a plastic bag and return it to the refrigerator for a few minutes. Kneading in the colour will make the paste warm and stringy, and it will be difficult to work with.

Many colours, particularly yellows and reds, will deepen on standing, so colour the paste a shade lighter than the desired finished colour.

An alternative method of colouring is to make all the flowers white, cream or a pale shade then petal dust to the desired shade when dry.

Petal dust is a powdered food colouring based on cornflour (cornstarch), which can be mixed in with the petal dust in small quantities to obtain a lighter shade.

Flower paste should be rolled as thinly as possible so that the petals will be translucent and natural looking. Paste can be rolled out on a thin film of white fat (shortening) or on a light dusting of cornflour. Experiment to find which one works best for you.

When doing a double frilling as in an orchid throat or carnation, the paste should be slightly thicker than usual or it will not frill successfully.

If using cornflour to dust the worksurface, place it in a square of butter muslin (cheesecloth) tied in a bag, or use a pepper pot for a miniature flour dredger.

MAKING SUGAR FLOWERS

1 *To soften petals use a cocktail stick (toothpick) and gently roll over the edge of the petal in a gentle motion. This is a very different principle from frilling as for the carnation.*

2 *Many flowers have to be frilled. Use a wooden cocktail stick (toothpick) and frill the outer edges of the petal with a firm rolling movement in a back and forward direction.*

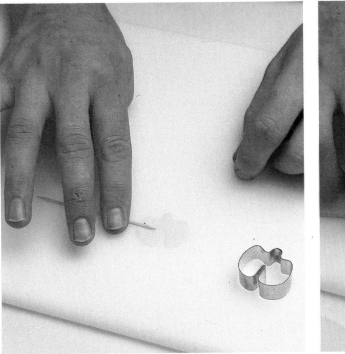

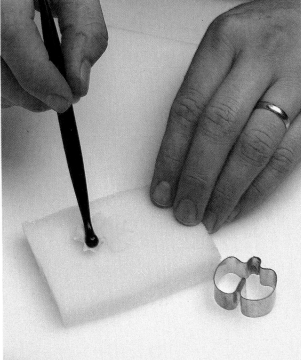

3 *Stick petals and attach to each other with fresh egg white using a small clean paintbrush.*

4 *Cup the petals on a piece of soft, sponge rubber using a dog bone or ball tool. The more pressure you apply, the more cupped the petal will become.*

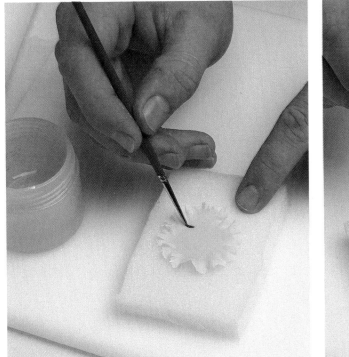

COLOURING FLOWERS

For certain flowers you will need a greater density of colour than dusting alone can give, for these you need to paint the petals. Mix a little petal dust or paste colour with some clear spirit (gin or vodka). Spirit is used for this purpose as it evaporates and dries quickly and does not soften the paste. However, mix only small quantities of colour as it too will evaporate while you work.

To get a soft overall effect on your sugar flowers you will need a soft round No4 brush. If a stronger density of colour is required on the outer edge of the petal only, a short, firm, flat brush should be used. Work with a gentle stroking movement from the outside of the petal to the inside. Using this principle, the spray carnation can have a contrasting colour on the petal edges.

SUGARPASTE ROSES

Sugarpaste roses are easy-to-make decorations for cakes and confectionery. If making coloured roses, knead the colour through the sugarpaste, then leave the paste to rest for about 15 minutes. Colouring the paste makes it very soft and stringy, but resting will return it to the original consistency.

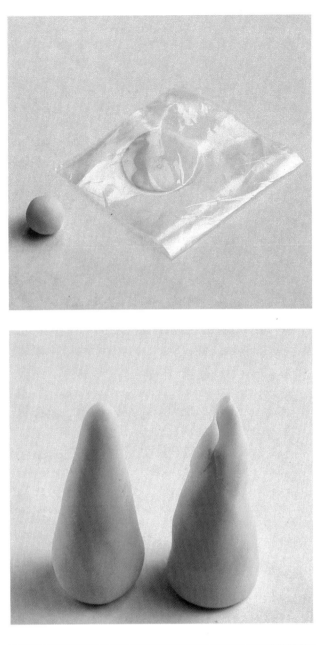

1   Take a pea-sized piece of paste and roll it in the palm of your hand. Flatten it between a folded piece of polythene by using your thumb and pulling away from yourself. Thin out about two-thirds of the paste, retaining the thicker base. This is the first petal.

2   Make a cone of sugarpaste and wrap the first petal completely around it. The cone should not be visible.

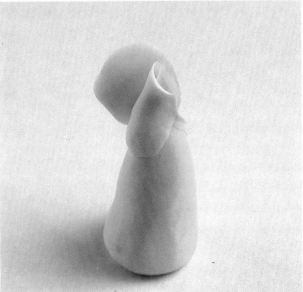

3   Make three more petals. Position one on the cone opposite the point where the first petal overlaps. Attach the left-hand side to the first petal and leave the right-hand side open. Repeat for the second petal, tucking each under and over.

175

4 *Attach the third petal by tucking it inside the second petal and over the top of the first. Waist in the base to establish the shape. For a rose bud, cut off the cone now using scissors or a sharp knife.*

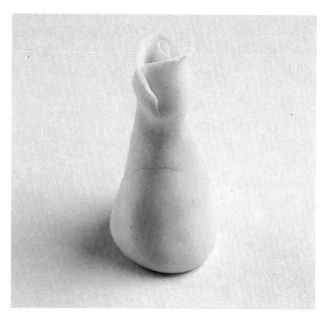

5 *If making a full rose, make another row of three petals, attaching them as before.*

6 *To make larger roses, continue adding petals, following the same formation. A fully-blown rose will have 19 petals. When the rose is the desired size, cut it off the cone using a sharp knife or scissors. Leave to dry thoroughly before placing roses on a cake.*

WIRED ROSE

The wired roses shown here are mainly used in sprays. To make realistic roses, start with flower paste in a fairly dark colour, then add a bit of white paste after each layer so that the rose is shaded from a dark centre cone to pale outer petals.

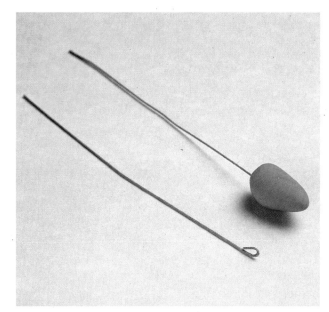

1 *Make a hook in the end of a piece of 26-gauge wire, dip into egg white, and mould a cone of flower paste around it.*

2 *Roll out some paste and cut two petals using a rose petal cutter. Slightly soften with a cocktail stick (toothpick). Wrap one petal around the cone and stick with a little egg white. Wrap the second petal around so that it sits in the flap of the first petal. Add some white to the coloured paste and roll out enough to cut three petals. Soften to frill slightly and cup by using a cranked ball tool. Wrap the petals around the first layer, tucking the first petal in the overlap of the previous row. The second petal goes in the flap of the first and the third petal goes in the flap of the second and on top of the first.*

3 *Cut five petals of the palest shade for the outer rows. Soften, cup slightly, and assemble as for the previous layers. Leave to dry for about 30 minutes.*

4   *Make the calyx by making a small hat shape from pale green paste. Roll out the edges, but keep the centre node. Cut as shown, thread onto the wire and mould slightly onto the base of the rose.*

5   *When dry petal dust the rose to bring out highlights. Dust the inside part of the calyx with white petal dust for a two-tone effect.*

This rose corsage has a wired rose as the focal point. The large pink rose is wired with an assortment of ivy, pulled blossom, gypsophila and ribbons.

178

SHALLOW DISH FLOWERS

ANEMONE

Anemones come in a range of colours: red, pink, cerise, violet, blue and cream. They are made with cutters and assembled by the shallow dish method. Use patty tins (pans) or polystyrene trays used to pack apples for shipping. When flowers and foliage are completely dry, assemble with the leaves arranged around the base of the flowers. If making a wired spray, attach to the main stem with a small amount of floristry tape.

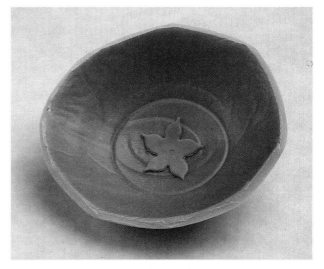

1 *Lightly grease the shallow dish with white vegetable fat (shortening). Roll out and cut a pale green calyx. If making wired anemones, make a slight cone in the base for the wire and insert wire.*

2 *Roll out the coloured paste very thinly and cut six petals using a rose petal cutter. Taking each petal in turn, soften the edges with a cocktail stick (toothpick), texture with a violet leaf veiner, then place on a dry sponge and cup slightly with a ball tool. Place upturned in an ice cube tray or something similar. When you have finished all six petals, start assembling with the first petal made.*

3 *Assemble on top of the calyx in the prepared shallow dish. Roll out another piece of paste and cut four or five more petals. Treat as Step 2, then assemble on top of the first layer, making a total of 10 or 11 petals. Leave to dry.*

179

4 *If making an anemone with white detail, mix white dusting powder with clear spirit and paint it in with a fine paintbrush. To make the stamen, place a small ball of paste on your forefinger and texture by pulling a small piece of tulle over it. Cover with black stamens and pieces of stamen cotton. Position in the centre of the petals. If not adding white detail, place stamen in the centre as soon as the flower is assembled.*

5 *Anemone foliage is made with a chrysanthemum leaf cutter. Cut using only the top half of the cutter, make as for variegated ivy, insert the wire, and leave to dry in a natural curve by supporting on foam.*

CHRISTMAS ROSE

Cut a green calyx and place in the shallow dish. Cut five white petals using a rose or Christmas rose cutter. Soften, cup and assemble as for the anemone. Position yellow stamens on a base in the centre. When dry, lightly dust green around the base and stamens.

PLUNGER-CUTTER FLOWERS

These little flowers are useful fillers as part of a larger bouquet, or may be used unwired to decorate cake tops and sides.

1 *Plunger blossom cutters come in several sizes, and plunger blossoms are quicker and easier to make than moulded flowers. First, roll out a small piece of paste very thinly. Place the plunger cutter on top of the paste and press down. Eject the flower onto a piece of sponge by pressing down the plunger.*

2 *Cup the flower using the small end of a ball tool or cranked ball tool. Cut out and cup about 20 flowers in this way. Make a hole in the centre of each blossom with a pin-ended modelling tool or with a large needle. Leave to dry for about 30 minutes.*

3 *Cut a few stamens in half and thread through the hole in the blossom. If making white flowers, use coloured stamens. Pipe a little royal icing under the stamen head and pull the stamen through so that it is fixed to the flower. Turn upside-down to dry.*

4 *Wire the blossom into sprays. Usually three large, four medium-sized and five small blossoms are included in a spray. Use fine strips of floristry tape to attach each blossom to 10 cm (4 in) long pieces of 28- or 30-gauge wire, and wire into a spray. Petal dust the finished sprays.*

FLOWERS MADE USING CUTTERS

Numerous varieties of flowers may be made from the many cutters now on the market. Cutters for flowers and foliage come in lots of sizes and makes, some metal and some plastic. Every manufacturer produces a slightly different shaped cutter for the same flower and they all make slightly different looking flowers. Unusual flowers may be made by modifying common cutters.

SPRAY CARNATION

Spray carnations are a very lovely, delicate flower to use on any celebration or wedding cake and can be finished in some interesting colour combinations.

Take a piece of 26-gauge mid-green wire, put a hook on one end and slip a piece of cotton or thread onto this, squash with pliers and wrap a piece of fine rose wire around the top piece. Using a thin piece of floristry tape, wrap around the top and tape down to the base of the wire.

Roll out some paste, but do not roll it until it is translucent as you would for the rose, as when double frilling it should be a fraction thicker. Cut out the carnation shape using the carnation cutter.

Using a sharp modelling knife, cut on the indentation and two or three times on the curve of each scallop. To frill the petal, take a cocktail stick (toothpick) and working with a firm rolling movement, start frilling the paste, keep it moving all the time so that it does not stick to the worksurface. Continue until frilled all the way around. Turn over onto a piece of thin foam, brush egg white all over the surface up to the frilling.

Thread the wire through the centre, fold in half, remove from sponge, brush egg white over the centre third of one side and bring the left-hand side third over; repeat on the other side by turning it over and bring from the side to the centre so it is an S shape if looked at from above. Squash firmly onto the wire.

Continue by rolling, cutting and frilling two further petals. These are turned over, brushed with

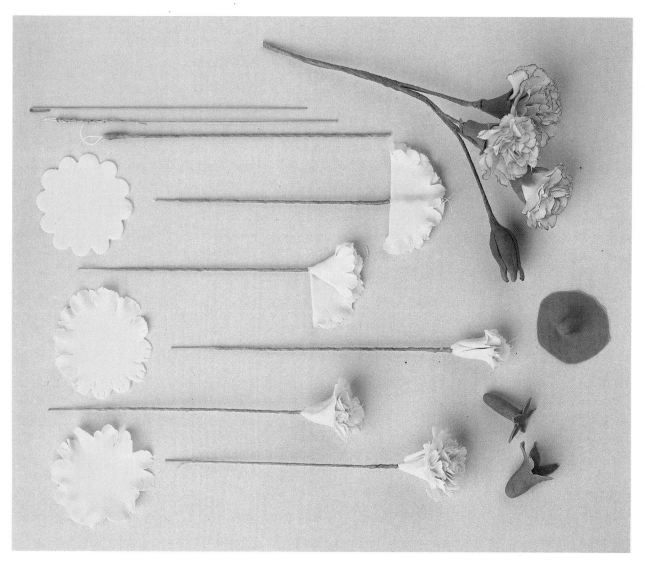

egg white and slid onto the wire. Hang upside-down supporting between your two thumbs and first fingers. Squash all around to get an even finish.

Make a small cone, known as a Mexican hat, rolling from the inside to the outside using a paintbrush. Cut out a calyx and then, as for pulled flowers, stick a wooden dowel down the centre to open it up. Slide the calyx up the wire and attach to the carnation with egg white.

To make the bud, surround a yellow cone with a piece of green paste and cut through the green using a modelling knife to reveal the yellow underneath. Place on a piece of wire. Dust the petals with a flat brush using a contrasting colour and wire with the bud into a spray.

MINIATURE CYMBIDIUM ORCHID

Miniature cymbidiums look very delicate on a tiny birthday cake or in a spray as a filler in conjunction with larger orchids. They are quite fiddly and quite time-consuming to make.

Make a tiny hook on a piece of 28-gauge wire. Place a small cone on one end, graduate its shape to form a bulbous tip. Vein on both sides and then bend the top over slightly. Roll out some pink paste and cut the throat petal. Frill the bottom edge and cup the two sides, then attach to the prepared column with egg white as shown. The sepals on this type of cutter are all in one; roll out some pink paste and cut out the petals. Vein each one down the centre. Cup one petal, then turn over and cup the other four, when you turn the petals over again they will curve backwards. Slide the throat into the centre of the petal sticking with a little egg white; leave until dry. Dust with a darker pink and paint a few delicate spots using petal dust mixed with clear spirit.

183

BASIC PULLED FLOWERS

Hand modelled or pulled flowers are made without cutters. The only basic equipment needed is a small wooden pointed stick, such as a cocktail stick (toothpick) or sharpened piece of dowelling, and a sharp modelling knife. The flower shown here is a basic five-petal blossom. The size of the finished flower is determined by the size of the piece of paste. Pulled blossom can also be made with four or six petals.

1 *Take a pea-sized piece of paste and make into a cone. Insert a wooden stick into the thick end of the cone. Use modelling knife to cut five equal-sized petals from the thick end of the cone.*

2 *Take the flower off the stick and open it up by taking each petal in turn and using these three motions:*
Squash: *squash the petal between your thumb and forefinger.*
Pinch: *pinch the end of the petal to make the edges slightly rounded.*
Pull: *soften and thin the petal by gently pulling the end between your thumb and forefinger, with the thumb on top and forefinger underneath.*
  Repeat the squash/pinch/pull motion on all five petals, keeping a uniform size.

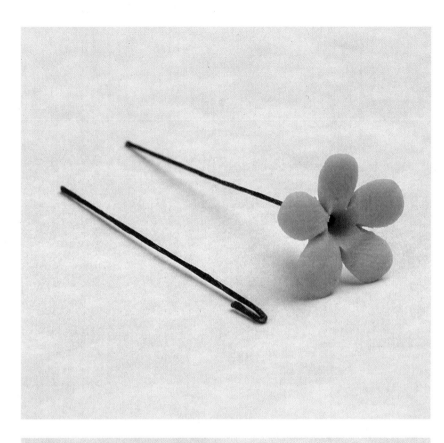

3 *Make a hook in the end of a piece of 28- to 30-gauge wire, dip into egg white and pull down through the centre of the flower. Mould the paste onto the wire.*

4 *When the blossom is dry, petal dust to the desired shade. These blossoms can be wired into sprays or used as filler flowers in other sprays.*

FREESIA

Make a dumb-bell shape in ivory paste and stick a dowel into one end. Cut into six equal parts; squash, pinch and pull and roll a cocktail stick (toothpick) over each petal. Place on a piece of sponge and cup each one stroking the ball tool from the outside to the inside of the flower. Push the ball or dog bone tool down the centre of the throat to stretch it slightly. Take a piece of 26-gauge mid-green wire, hook and dip in egg white and thread through the throat. Take a small ball of paste and place inside the flower to act like a plug to stop it from sliding down the wire. Using a cocktail stick (toothpick) make a small hole in the plug and fold together three 2.5 cm (1 in) pieces of cotton or stamen cotton and push the folded ends into the hole. Using the thumb and first fingers of both hands squash slightly. Move three alternate petals inwards and others outwards, squash just below the petals. To make sure the centre three stay in position, the outer three are then gently eased up to sit as a second row on top of the first three petals.

The buds are made in various sizes, the smallest are just tiny cones placed on wire and rolled down between the fingers to form a long, elegant bud.

Once dry, just dust with pink or any other appropriate petal dust, as freesias come in a wide range of colours. A little green petal dust is brushed into the centre and around the base of the flower. The buds are lightly dusted all over with green while the twisted buds are half green and half pink. You will need graduated flowers as well as buds to make a spray.

Mix a little green food colouring with some clear spirit and paint a calyx on each bud and flower. Paint a small single leaf shape on either side using a fine paintbrush and allow to dry. Assemble starting with the smallest bud and placing the others to the right, then to the left all the way down.

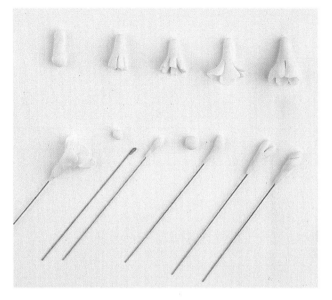

186

BLUEBELL

Colour some paste bluish-mauve and roll into a ball. Mould into a dumb-bell shape, stick a dowel into one end and cut six petals. Place each petal on a piece of sponge and cup using a ball tool stick, then insert a ball tool up into the centre of the flower to make a bulbous cavity. Using tweezers, pinch the flower to produce a ribbed effect on the side.

Tape two white stamen ends onto a piece of wire, and wrap round extra tape to stop the wire coming back through the flower. Thread the wire and stamens through the flower. The buds are made by making a small cone, and then pinching with tweezers.

Brush with a mixture of blue and violet dusting powder. Tape the buds and flowers onto a main stem as shown starting with a bud in the centre then setting another to the left then the next to the right and so on. You can make a long spray by using five to seven buds and five to seven flowers. Bluebells look attractive bunched together with other spring flowers as a cake centrepiece.

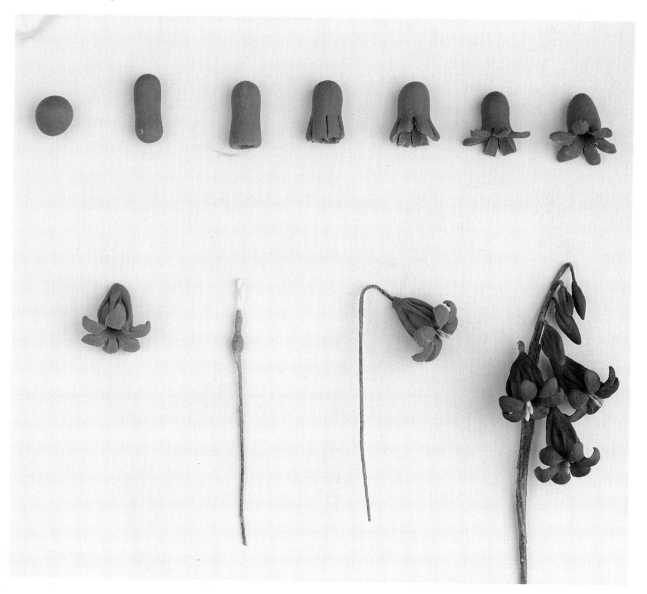

FOLIAGE AND FILLER FLOWERS

Many different leaf shapes can be made from florist's tape. Leaves made from tape are particularly useful and very effective when used to represent the foliage of such flowers as mimosa, fuchsia, jasmine and carnations when these flowers are wired into sprays. The foliage of these flowers when made from flower paste may shatter when wired into complicated sprays, but making foliage from florist's tape allows the sprays to be wired tightly without causing breakages.

To make florist's tape foliage, use sharp scissors to cut out a realistic shape and size for the leaf. The leaves can either be used wired or unwired in the sprays.

IVY LEAF

Ivy leaves are useful foliage suitable for year round use. They are, however, particularly useful for Christmas cakes. The ones shown are variegated ivy but the principle is the same for all foliage.

Take a piece of pale ivory-coloured paste and roll into a ball. Squash, and roll with a paintbrush, retaining a thicker part at one end for the wire. Cut out the ivy leaf positioning the base at thicker part as shown; hold firmly between your thumb and first finger and insert a 28-gauge wire that has first been hooked and dipped in egg white. Place on an ivy leaf or violet leaf veiner or use a real ivy leaf. Vein on both sides. Run a cocktail stick (toothpick) over the edge to soften slightly. Place on a sponge and vein the centre of the leaf using a veining tool or cocktail stick. Pinch the bottom slightly and leave to dry. When dry, dust the back green, then work the variegation by using two shades of green. Brush the lighter shade on first using a flat paintbrush and brushing from the centre to the outside of the leaf, then using a darker shade, dust on top of the lighter colour, again working from the centre out towards the edges.

GYPSOPHILA

Gypsophila is a popular inclusion for wedding sprays, as it helps to soften the effect of brightly coloured flowers. Make hooks in the ends of 30-gauge covered wire, dip into egg white, and mould tiny pieces of white paste over each hook. For each flower, squash a small sausage of paste between your thumb and forefinger. Roll with a paintbrush, then frill with a cocktail stick (toothpick). Put some egg white down the frilled edge, place the paste-covered wire at one end and roll up to make the flowers, which should look a little like miniature carnations. Wire several flowers and buds into a spray and use a fine paintbrush dipped in green food colouring to paint on the calyxes.

MIMOSA

Mimosa looks attractive when used as a filler in sugar flower sprays, particularly sprays of spring flowers. Colour the flower paste yellow and make into pea-sized balls. For each ball, make a hook in the end of a piece of covered 30-gauge wire. Thread through the paste and secure it onto the wire. Dip the paste into egg white, and then dip into yellow petal dust or coloured sugar. Arrange into a realistic shape and tape together several flowers. Make the foliage from floristry tape.

Many dozens of flowers can be made using the techniques shown and once the technique is mastered you should be able to look at almost any flower and be able to make it by deciding which of the skills will be necessary to use. The flowers covered in this chapter may be used in a variety of sprays and floral arrangements. The following provide just a few ideas to get you started.

DECORATING IDEAS

BABY'S BOOTIES

A pair of small china baby's booties filled with pastel-tipped petal blossom would be a suitable gift for a new arrival or for a christening cake. Fill the booties with white sugarpaste; make some figure-of-eight double loops in lemon and white. Place the ribbons in position, then arrange an assortment of sizes of basic five-petal blossom and buds in the booties using a pair of tweezers. Tie two lemon bows and stick these on to the front of the booties with royal icing or a rubber-based glue.

SILVER VASE

This flowering vase is filled with dozens of pulled blossoms and buds. Make five identical legs and wire into a posy with double figure-of-eight loops and stick into a silver vase. This would be an ideal top decoration for a three tier wedding cake. The principle for wiring is like the reverse S spray page 192.

KNIFE

For a spectacular birthday or wedding cake, decorate the knife with a spray of sugar flowers to match the spray on the cake. Attach to the knife with florist's wire, then cover the wire with ribbons to match the spray.

OVAL WEDDING CAKE

30 cm (12 in) and 25 cm (10 in) oval rich fruit cakes,
marzipanned and sugarpasted
35 cm (14 in) oval silver cake board
25 cm (10 in) thin oval silver cake card or 28 cm (11 in)
cake board
4 metres (4 yds) 1 cm (½ in) plain lilac ribbon
4 metres (4 yds) 5 mm (¼ in) deep purple ribbon
4 metres (4 yds) 5 mm (¼ in) lilac polka dot ribbon
30 ml (2 tablespoons) royal icing
375 g (12 oz) flower paste
Pink and violet food colourings
Pearl stamens

Measure and fit all three ribbons around the base of each cake. Fit the plain lilac ribbon at the base, secured with a stainless pin. Repeat to fit deep purple ribbon next, then polka dot ribbon last. Make 16 tiny purple bows and 16 tiny polka dot bows from remaining ribbon. Place these bows in pairs at intervals around the base of the cakes, alternating the colours. Secure with a bead of royal icing.

Divide flower paste into three and colour pale, medium and dark purple to match the ribbons. Make 15 hand-moulded roses using dark flower paste for centres, then medium to light petals on the outside. Leave to dry on foam sponge until hard. Make 13 pulled blossom flowers with light and medium coloured flower paste and pearl stamens. Use the remaining coloured flower paste to make tiny flowers using plunger blossom cutters and stamens (see pages 174, 184 and 181 for further details).

When dry, wire the tiny blossoms together into 18 sprays. Make small loops of ribbon and wire carefully. Place small cake on top of large cake so back edges are level. The boards may be left in position or removed. Arrange some of the sugar flowers, ribbon loops and sugar flower sprays on top of small cake. Using remaining sugar flowers, ribbons and sprays, make four separate sugar flower arrangements at intervals around the top edge of the large oval cake. Secure with royal icing and leave to set. Separate cakes carefully and place in cake boxes until required.

Re-assemble on the day.

Above: Making hand moulded roses.

Frosted Pink 21st Cake

25 cm (10 in) oval rich or light fruit cake, marzipanned
   and royal iced
30 cm (12 in) silver oval cake board
2 metres (2 yds) 1 cm (½ in) white fancy ribbon
2 metres (2 yds) 5 mm (¼ in) pink polka dot ribbon
60 ml (4 tablespoons) royal icing
Twinkle pink petal dust
Rose pink food colouring
250 g (8 oz) flower paste
Cornflour (cornstarch)
Large and small pearl centre stamens
21st silver key emblem

Measure and fit white ribbon around base and in
centre of cake. Trim and secure with a little royal
icing. Fit polka dot ribbon over the two bands of
white ribbon, secure with icing. Tie two large bows
with long ends and fit to front and back of cake on
centre band of ribbon with a little icing. Brush top
of cake with petal dust to coat evenly, then dust cake
board.

   Divide flower paste into three pieces and colour
three distinct shades of pink with rose pink food
colouring. Roll out dark pink sugarpaste thinly on
a lightly cornfloured (cornstarched) surface. Using
a large five-petal flower cutter, cut out nine large
flowers, pierce a hole in centre and thread through
a large pearl stamen, secure with a tiny bead of royal
icing. Repeat to make 18 large flowers and leave to
dry on a piece of foam sponge. Using medium pink
petal paste, make 10 medium-sized flowers using a
daisy cutter and pearl stamens, and use the pale pink
flower paste to make 30 small flowers using a large
plunger blossom cutter and small pearl stamens. To
make the tiny flowers, use smaller plunger blossom
cutters and all three shades of flower paste and small
pearl centres. When dry, wire tiny and small flowers
together to make six sprays.

   Using a large plain writing tube in a paper piping
bag, fill with some royal icing, fold down top and
pipe a thick line of icing two-thirds of the way round
top edge, leaving the two ends clear. Leave in a dry
place to set. Arrange the flowers and sprays on each
end of the cake, secure each carefully with a little
royal icing. Place '21' emblem in centre of cake on
a line of royal icing. Leave in a dry place to set.

1 *Make large flowers, cut out stamen, leave to dry.*

2 *Making small and medium flowers, pressing out petals
and fitting stamen. Wiring blossoms into sprays.*

RIBBONS IN CAKE DECORATING

Ribbons have many different uses in cake decorating. As well as being part of nearly every sugar flower spray, they are used to cover cake boards, trim cakes, and as part of top decorations. Ribbon is made from many different materials – paper, silk, velvet, nylon, polyester – and comes in different widths. For cake decorating, ribbons in widths of 3 mm – 2.5 cm (⅛ – 1 in) are most commonly used.

CHOOSING RIBBONS

For covering cake boards and banding cakes, almost any ribbon which looks good can be used. However, ribbon for use in sugar flower sprays must be able to hold its shape. To see if a ribbon is suitable for sprays, take the end of a reel and fold it over to make a loop. If the loop holds it shape and the ribbon supports its own weight, then the ribbon is suitable for sprays. Some ribbons, particularly those made of nylon, will not hold a shape, and then the loops in sprays will look flat and messy.

Try to use double-faced ribbon, which means that it is shiny on both sides. Single-faced ribbon has a matt and a shiny face, and it will not look as good when tied in bows or made into loops. Buy ribbon with bound edges, as unbound edges may fray.

BOWS

Miniature bows are easy to make using fine-pointed tweezers. Take the ribbon and make a small loop with a tail of about 5 cm (2 in) in the front. Hold the loop with the tweezers in your right hand. Take the excess piece over the right-hand side of the tweezers, and make a complete circle. Hold with your fingers and release the tweezers. There will be a small loop on the right. Put the tweezers through the loop and pull through the ribbon from the other side. Pull the two loops tight and cut the tails. These miniature bows are often used on top of frills.

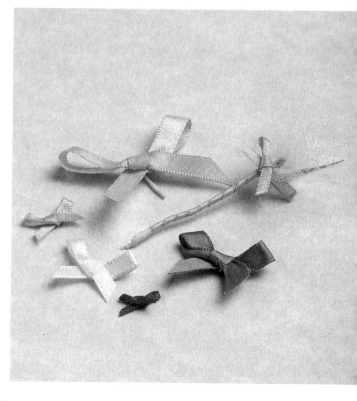

REVERSED S-CURVE SPRAY

This reversed S-curve has been made using miniature flowers. You will need five miniature orchids, 18 assorted-sized pulled blossom, six frilled blossom, nine buds, seven small ivy leaves and some ribbon.

1 *Start by making the upper leg of the spray. Take a single bud, then tape in another two buds. Start adding pulled blossom, frilled blossom, an ivy leaf and finish with a miniature orchid. Make an identical leg for the bottom, but work so that the spray is a mirror image of the first one.*

2 *Wire together a small posy, leaving two cavities for the legs of the spray.*

194

3 *Tape in the ribbon loops to fill out the spray and give a rounded, even shape.*

4 *Tape in the legs, and use some blossom as filler flowers.*

FILIGREE AND LACE

Filigree and lace work is not for the beginner as competence in basic piping skills is required. Lace pieces attached to a cake produce a very fine and delicate effect which is perfect for a very special cake. Filigree work can produce a similar effect and can also be used to create centrepieces such as caskets and Christening cribs.

The two cakes show very simple lace and filigree work. The lilac lace pieces which stand out from the top and decorate the bottom of the lower cake do look pretty while being created from a very simple basic shape. The filigree butterflies are very pretty, but also very fragile – always make plenty of spares as these cakes can be easily damaged when handling.

COLOURING ICING

Most filigree and lace work is white but it is possible to make it in a colour to match the cake, table decorations, dresses, etc.

When colouring icing for this type of work, always use powder colours. Most paste and syrup colours contain glycerine, and liquid colours will stop the icing drying.

Make sure you colour enough icing to complete the work, as matching colours later can be difficult.

Mix the powder into the icing, cover with a damp cloth or lid and leave the colour to develop for about ten minutes. Several colours, especially yellow, will dry darker than they appear in the bowl. Be careful when using blue and mauve, as these tend to fade quickly when dry.

Let piped pieces dry, then store away from bright sunlight so the colour does not fade.

Several colours can be used to pipe one piece of work. This takes time as three to five bags of different coloured icing are used on a tiny piece of lace.

An alternative to colouring icing is to make white or pale cream pieces and shade them with petal dust or lustre colour when dry. Dust the colour on the dried work with a No3 or 4 soft paintbrush. This is best done on waxed paper, which will stop the piece from moving about. Once dusted, remove from paper.

Because royal icing absorbs moisture from the atmosphere, piped lace and filigree pieces are sensitive to the weather. On humid days the work can become crumbly and break easily. Therefore fine work such as attaching tiny pieces of sugar lace to a cake should be done on as dry a day as possible.

Lace and filigree can be made well in advance. Once dry, store between sheets of tissue paper. Do not use cotton wool as the points can catch and break. Store pieces in a cake box or other cardboard box, not sealed in an airtight tin or plastic container. Store the container in an airing cupboard or near a heat source. Try to keep at a constant temperature. Storage in a room heated by day and cold at night can cause breakages to fine work.

Most lace pieces are about the size of a fingernail. When designing these small lace pieces, check the scale. Make sure they will not look too large or too small. If being attached around the side of a cake, calculate the size carefully so that a gap or an overlap does not occur.

There are two main types of lace pieces. The type with a straight top line is easier to handle and to attach to the cake. The second type, freestyle (for example the bow), is not as strong. It is attached with two small dots of icing instead of a line.

MAKING LACE PIECES

Successful lace piping takes a lot of practice, especially when making many pieces of identical lace. Choose a design with several joins to begin with, and make a multiple template, as shown here. It is worth using good quality paper or card, as the template can then be used many times. Have paper and several filled piping bags ready.

1 *Draw half a piece of lace on a piece of paper using a pencil. Copy the half piece onto tracing paper. Turn over and transfer design back to the first piece of paper, ending up with a whole lace piece. The reason for the tracing is to ensure that the two sides stay identical.*

2 *Make a tracing of the whole piece and transfer to thick paper or thin card. Repeat design to make 8 – 50 lace pieces. Once traced, go over with a pen to make a permanent template.*

3 *Stick a piece of waxed paper over the template. Use a small piping bag fitted with a No0 or 00 tube. Start with the straight line and work towards the pointed end.*

4 *Repeat until all the pieces on the template have been piped. Transfer carefully to a flat surface to dry.*

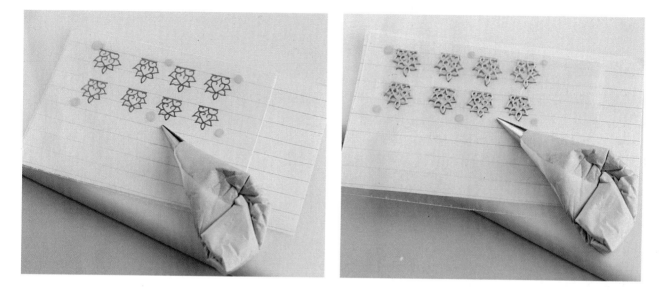

5. *Dry lace pieces ready for attaching to the cake.*

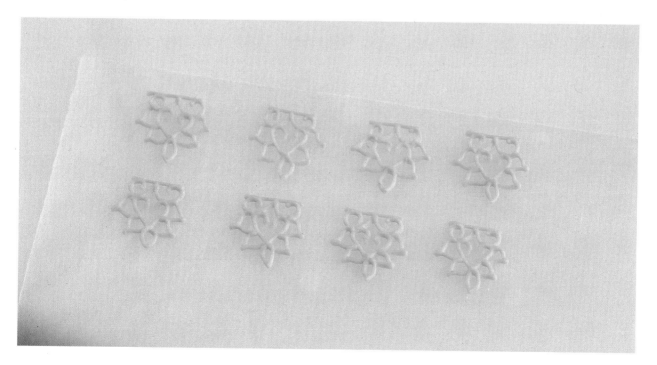

LACE DESIGNS

Remember that lace which looks simple may not always be the easiest to do. Lace which has several short lines and joins will be stronger than that which has fewer lines. Always pipe more lace than the design of the cake calls for. If the cake is to be delivered, always take some extra lace on waxed paper and a filled piping bag wrapped in plastic as lace often gets damaged or drops off.

Always use freshly made royal icing to attach and pipe lace. Old icing will not produce strong lace, and will not hold it firmly on the cake.

Templates for design on the following pages can be found on page 249.

TWO-TONE LACE

These two- and three-tone lace pieces are stunning but they will take longer to pipe than single-colour lace as you must keep changing icing bags. Have all the bags filled and ready before you begin. Colour the icing with petal dust.

PIPING CURVED LACE

Lace can be dried on a former or over a length of pipe or dowel to make it curve.

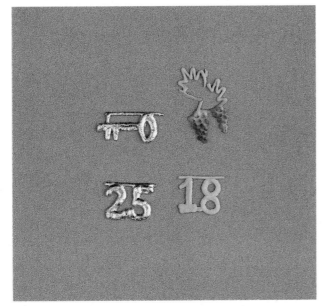

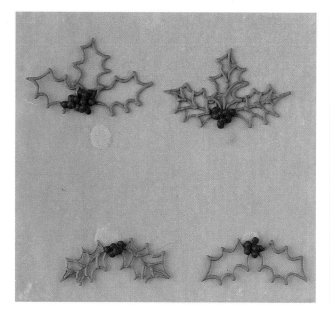

1 *Holly wreath lacework.*

2 *Holly leaves, use in conjunction with wreath for a sophisticated Christmas cake.*

3 *Intricate lacework from traditional design.*

4 *Two-tone lacework.*

5 *Small two-tone designs.*

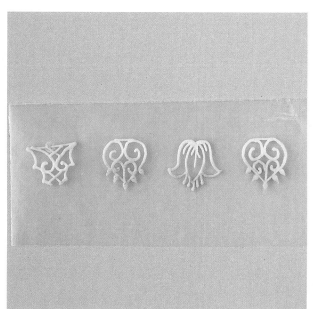

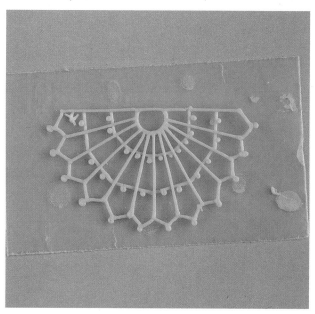

FILIGREE FLOWERS

In filigree work, an outline is piped or run out to act as a border and support. The area inside is then piped with various designs and patterns, from the easiest cornelli work to complicated designs. Filigree can be used for the total decoration on a cake: side pieces, wings and centrepiece.

Filigree work can be used to create all kinds of lovely flowers, such as the pansy and daffodil shown here. Use white icing and dust with colour when dry, or colour the icing with petal dust before piping. The flowers can be placed individually on a cake, or they can be wired into sprays. Filigree flowers are extremely fragile, so take care when wiring.

DAFFODIL

Pipe three of each of the two template petals onto waxed paper. Place the broader petals *over* a curve and the three other petals *in* a curve. Grease a piping tube and pipe the trumpet onto it. Remove all six petals from the paper when dry. Hold piping tube in front of heat source to remove trumpet. Pipe a small circle of yellow royal icing on waxed paper. Place the other three petals in position curving upwards. Put trumpet in the centre with royal icing. Add five stamens; let dry.

Dust trumpet with orange petal dust. To use in a spray, or as shown, stick a wire and floristry tape leaf behind flower.

PANSY

Pipe the petals on waxed paper as shown. Set the top two petals *over* a curve. Set the other three *into* a curve. Once dry, assemble on waxed paper with a little royal icing. Let it dry, then dust mauve and yellow.

Daffodil – pipe three of each petal.

Pansy – pipe one of each petal.

Trellis Work

See page 250 for template. A heart is a simple popular shape for any occasion.

1 *Make two halves. Pipe outline with a No1 tube, pipe rose design followed by trellis with a No1, then the scalloped edge with a No0.*

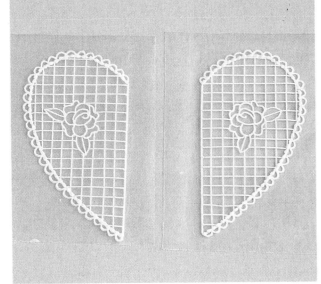

2 *Pipe a line down centre of cake with a No2 tube. Place two halves in position touching. Support with foam and dry for two hours. Remove foam.*

3 *Place 3 mm (⅛ in) ribbon down centre to neaten the join. Attach a few pink flowers to cake. Pipe some green leaves and a small dove.*

FILIGREE WITH TULLE

Filigree can be used to good effect when piped directly onto tulle. The tulle is so fine it becomes hardly noticeable against the piped filigree, but does help to keep the filigree together for shapes and formed filigree that would otherwise collapse. Remember that items made from tulle are inedible.

FILIGREE CASKET

Using the templates provided on page 248 cut out the necessary shapes from tulle. The easy way to do this is to make a tracing of the shapes and place this over the tulle, then cut through the pattern and the tulle at the same time. Pin the tulle quite taut over a drawing of the shapes using long, glass-headed pins. A cake board is ideal for pressing pins into.

1   *Pipe filigree over the tulle with yellow royal icing and a No1 tube. Edge all shapes with straight piped lines, and edge the curves with a tiny shell still using a No1 tube. Also make the semi-circle section, outline the shape with a No1 tube and flood in with yellow run-icing.*

2   *Secure the longest of the two straight pieces onto a curved former to dry, a ring of plastic rainwater piping is ideal.*

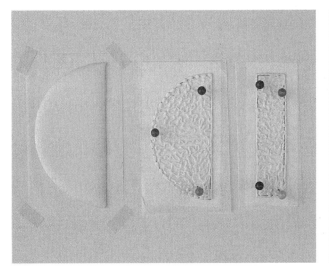

3   *When all the parts are dry, assemble them as shown, sticking together with royal icing. Small pieces of polystyrene may be required to support the sides until dry.*

4   *Make an arrangement of small sugar flowers and attach these inside the casket. You could use piped, royal-iced flowers as shown or cutter-type flowers made from paste. Attach two lids as shown, leaving a space between each. Edge the casket with a picot dot edging piped in yellow icing using a No0 tube.*

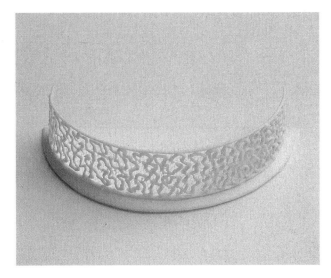

FILIGREE CRADLE

1   *Using the same method as described for the tulle casket, make the necessary pieces for the cradle as shown using the templates provided on page 248.*

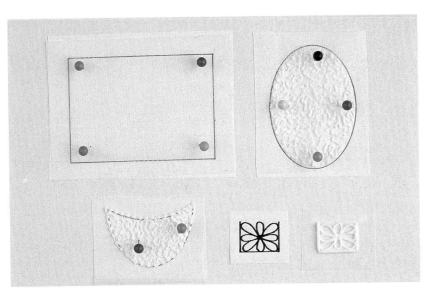

2   *Shape the base of the cradle over a curved former. The picture shows a cardboard tube taped to a photographic slide box.*

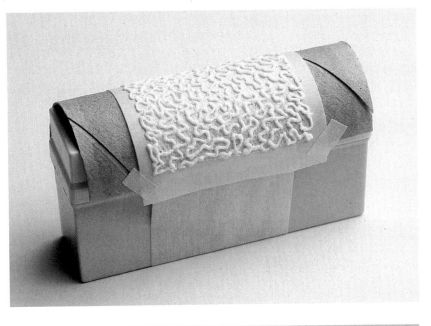

3   *Assemble the sections of the cradle as shown, edging the filigree with a tiny pink-coloured icing shell. Line the inside of the cradle with cotton wool and place on a small ball of flesh-coloured marzipan or sugarpaste for the baby's head. Rest the filigree cover over the baby. A few bows can also be attached.*

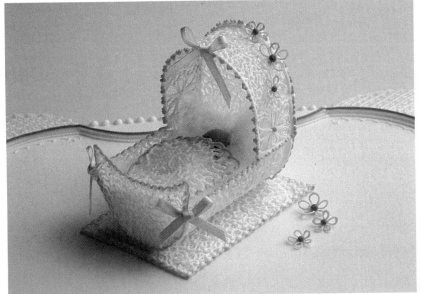

BUTTERCREAM FILIGREE AND LACE

Buttercream can be used to pipe lace and filigree designs onto cakes, just as for royal icing. Many of the designs shown can be adapted for buttercream work.

Because buttercream does not set hard, it is not possible to use it for freestanding objects, or for lace which stands away from the cake. However, designs can be piped onto the surface of the cake and lace can be piped around the top, sides or cake board.

Use buttercream which is stiffer than coating consistency. Piping bags for buttercream work can be larger than those used for royal icing, but because the heat of your hand changes the consistency of the icing, it is better to use several small bags. Colour the buttercream with paste colours, as liquid colourings will thin the icing. Although it is possible to pipe very fine work in buttercream, the very smallest piping tubes are difficult to use. A No0 or No1 tube is the smallest tube which will give successful results.

When piping buttercream lace or filigree on a buttercream-covered cake, lightly mark the design on the cake first, using a scriber or other sharp object. Remember that it is always possible to smooth over the buttercream if the design is not successful the first time. However, coloured icing will mark the surface of the cake and will not be easy to scrape off.

Buttercream lace is piped directly onto the cake, rather than on waxed paper, so it may be difficult to duplicate the same design several times. If you do not feel confident to pipe freehand designs, choose a lace pattern which is fairly simple and trace it onto paper several times and use the tracings to scribe the design onto the cake.

Filigree in coloured buttercream can be piped onto a sugarpasted cake, or onto a cake which has been covered with melted chocolate and allowed to dry.

Never store a buttercream cake in the refrigerator, as the icing will sweat and the colours will run. Buttercream does not keep for very long, and the cake should be eaten soon after decorating.

USING TEMPLATES
Cut out a simple template such as crescent shape, use this for further practice. Templates can be very useful on actual cakes when piping filigree patterns, you can experiment with them on cake tops and sides to produce many interesting effects.

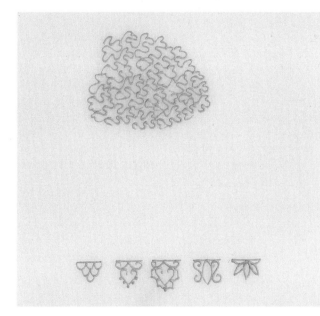

DECORATING IDEAS

MOTHER'S DAY CAKE

A delightful cake for Mother's Day. Bake a shallow cake to give this modern appearance. Coat the cake in cream-coloured royal icing and edge with lilac-coloured shells using a No44 tube. Chocolate-coloured icing is used to edge the shells on the cake top and to pipe a filigree edge around the coated base board. Position the filigree casket on the cake top and pipe the inscription using chocolate-coloured icing and a No1 tube. A narrow cream-coloured ribbon and bow complete the cake.

TRELLIS-WORK HEART CAKE

Make trellis-work heart and position on a pale green royal iced cake. Divide cake top into eight. Pipe eight pairs of scrolls overpiped with trellis in darker pink. Add tiny bows. Let dry and place in position. Pipe a shell around base with a No43 tube and dropped lines with a No1. Finish with scalloped rope lines around shells and a wavy line around the edge.

BUTTERCREAM FILIGREE CHOCOLATE CAKE

Cover a square cake with two coats of melted chocolate. Use a comb scraper on the sides. Leave to set. Make a pattern of greaseproof (waxed) paper from the template. Use a scriber or hat pin to transfer the pattern onto the top of the cake. Use green and peach buttercream, each with a No2 tube, to pipe the design. Sides and edges are piped freehand. Do not store cake in the refrigerator as the chocolate will form beads of moisture and the buttercream will separate.

STRAWBERRY CAKE

Prepare the cake by layering with strawberry-flavoured buttercream. Coat the cake in pink-coloured, strawberry-flavoured cream. Comb-scrape the sides and chill the cake. Mark the cake top into four sections using the back of a knife. Place a food cutter in the centre of the cake and sprinkle some sieved jap biscuit crumb or fine nibbed nuts into the shape of the cutter, remove the cutter carefully. Next pipe straight lines of white buttercream using a 5 mm (¼ in) plain piping tube. The lines should start at the edge of the centre dressing and come out to the edge of the cake. Pipe filigree in the four sections, using pink buttercream. Then pipe a wavy line on the white buttercream lines using chocolate buttercream or melted chocolate thickened with a few drops of cold water. Finish the top edge and the base with pink buttercream shells piped with a No44 tube. Model four strawberries from marzipan (see page 231) and mount them on discs of chocolate, piped onto waxed paper. Position the strawberry decorations on the cake.

From top to bottom: Trellis-work heart cake, buttercream filigree chocolate cake and strawberry cake.

LACE CAKE

20 cm (8 in) fruit cake, marzipanned and royal iced in white
on a 25 cm (10 in) silver drum board
lilac 500 g (1 lb/3½ Cups) royal icing
1 metre (1 yd) 1 cm (½ in) lace ribbon
5 purchased ribbon roses

Colour half the royal icing lilac. Using thin card draw the lace shape 1 cm (½ in) long and 1 cm (½ in) high ten times leaving plenty of space between each shape. Fix a strip of waxed paper over the top and using a No1 tube and lilac icing carefully trace the outline. When all the pieces have been piped place on a flat surface to dry. Continue to pipe further strips of pieces making plenty of spares in case of breakage. Leave to dry completely.

Using a 10 cm (4 in) disc of card, pipe a small ring of S and C scrolls using a No2 tube and white icing. Place dots between the scrolls with a No1 tube and lilac icing. Using a No3 tube pipe white bulbs round the top edge only. Ensuring that the lace pieces are completely dry peel off and attach to the cake by gently pushing the straight edge into the soft icing so that the lace projects evenly around the cake. Pipe

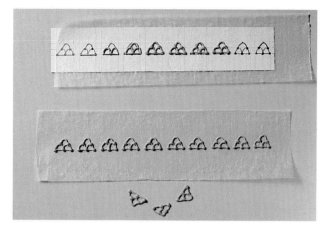

Making lace pieces (see template on page 250).

dots of lilac icing between the bulbs.

Pipe another row of bulbs around the base of the cake using a No3 tube and white icing. Lay lace pieces on the board just touching the wet icing so that they hold in position. Add lilac dots between the bulbs.

Attach ribbon to the sides of the cake and place the bought decorations on the top securing both with dots of royal icing.

BUTTERFLY PETAL CAKE

20 cm (8 in) petal cake, marzipanned and royal iced in blue
on a 25 cm (10 in) silver drum board
750 g (1½ lb/5¼ Cups) royal icing
Blue food colouring
1 metre (1 yd) white ribbon

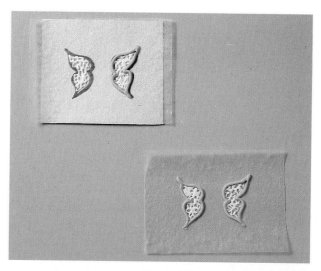

To make the butterflies, colour about one-third of the icing blue. Trace the butterfly wings onto a piece of card and cover with waxed paper. Thin down the white icing and use to fill a bag fitted with a No0 tube. Fill in the centre portion of each wing with cornelli work (see page 113), then while this icing is still soft, pipe the outer blue outline using a No2 tube. Ensure that the blue line touches cornelli work in as many places as possible. Leave to dry.

Peel the paper off the butterflies very carefully. Make a card former and place a small piece of waxed paper in the centre. Pipe a body for the butterfly in white icing using a No2 tube. Carefully insert the wings into the body while still soft and leave to dry.

Make a 10 cm (4 in) template the same shape as the cake and place on centre of the cake. Pipe a line with a No2 tube and white icing following the line of the template. Pipe cornelli work with a No0 tube inside this line.

With a No44 tube and using white icing pipe a shell edge on the top and bottom of the cake. Change to a No1 tube and pipe a further line following the shape of the shells. While the icing is still soft fix the butterflies into position. Place the ribbon around the sides of the cake and fix with dots of icing. Pipe a line of shells in each of the grooves using the No44 tube and white icing, as shown.

1 *Piping filigree butterfly wings (see template on page 250).*

2 *Adding wings to piped body in paper frame.*

211

CHOCOLATE

Working with chocolate is unlike working in any of the other materials covered in the book so far, although several of the skills can be adapted for use with this popular decoration. Chocolate can be coloured, cutout, curled, moulded and piped into filigree and lace pieces or even runout to create shapes and characters. The use of such ideas is not, of course, restricted to cake decoration – they look great on cheesecakes, topping mousses and decorating sweet tarts.

The cakes featured are all Christmas cakes, not everyone wants a rich fruit cake and sometimes if a cake is required at short notice one of these would be perfect.

WORKING WITH CHOCOLATE

There are two types of chocolate for use in sugarcraft – baker's chocolate and couverture. Baker's chocolate, also called compound chocolate, is much easier to work with, but does not have as good a flavour as couverture, which is the purest form of chocolate. Both types are available in plain (semi-sweet), milk and white forms.

BAKER'S CHOCOLATE

Baker's chocolate is available from most supermarkets and sugarcraft suppliers in slabs or buttons. It differs from couverture in that most of the cocoa butter has been removed and replaced with a vegetable fat (shortening), eliminating the need for tempering.

To melt baker's chocolate place in the top of a double saucepan over hand-hot water and stir until melted. Heat to a temperature of 38–43°C (100–110°F), or until completely smooth, if not using a thermometer. If the chocolate gets too hot it may have fat bloom – white streaks. White sugar bloom may appear if the chocolate is too cool. Never allow steam or moisture to get in contact with the chocolate, or it will thicken and become unusable.

Baker's chocolate can be placed in the refrigerator after it has set to hasten contraction.

If you are new to chocolate work, then begin with the baker's chocolate as it is the easiest to handle.

COUVERTURE

Chocolate work done with couverture will be smooth and glossy, and the flavour will be better than baker's chocolate. However, couverture has to be tempered before use. Couverture is available from sugarcraft suppliers and some specialist food shops. Most bars of dessert (dark) chocolate are made by a different process and are not suitable for chocolate work, so check before you use a new make of chocolate.

There are many different methods for tempering couverture, which involves heating and then cooling the chocolate to a precise temperature so that the fat in the cocoa butter crystallizes. Well-tempered chocolate will have a high gloss and snap when set. For all the work in this book baker's chocolate is recommended for simplicity.

TO THICKEN CHOCOLATE FOR PIPING

Melt 125 g (4 oz/4 squares) chocolate and add 2 – 3 drops of glycerine to thicken. Chocolate with added glycerine will start to set quickly. If it sets in the bowl it cannot be remelted, so only thicken a small amount at a time.

COLOURED CHOCOLATE

Heat a saucepan about one-third full of water until hot, but not boiling. Chop white chocolate into small pieces and place in a bowl. Stand the bowl over the pan of water and gently stir with a wooden spoon until the chocolate has melted. The white chocolate will not be as runny as melted plain (semi-sweet) chocolate as it melts at a lower temperature, about 44°C (110°F).

White chocolate may be quite granular even when properly melted. Smooth chocolate may be obtained by standing a second bowl in hot water and pouring the chocolate into this through a fine metal sieve. Take care to wipe the bottom of the first bowl after it has been lifted from the water as any drops of water falling into the melted chocolate will cause it to thicken and spoil. For this reason, do not use water-based liquid colouring.

Ladle a little chocolate into a plastic cup and add a little powdered colouring. Mix thoroughly until the chocolate is evenly blended. Place the coloured chocolate back in the bowl of melted chocolate and mix until the desired shade is reached.

CHOCOLATE CURLS AND CUTOUTS

Chocolate curls can be used to decorate cakes or desserts. They are the traditional decoration on a Black Forest Gâteau. Pour the melted chocolate onto a marble slab or follow the method here. Handle the curls carefully, as they are fragile and melt easily.

Simple designs can be made by making chocolate cutouts using biscuit (cookie) or aspic cutters, or by cutting the chocolate with a sharp knife around a template.

1. Pour the melted chocolate onto greaseproof (waxed) paper. Pick up and drop the paper several times, or spread the chocolate backwards and forwards with a palette knife until it just sets. Be sure that the chocolate is smooth and an even thickness without any air bubbles, or the cutouts will not look attractive and may break.

2. Use a sharp knife held at a 45 degree angle to the chocolate. Shave the chocolate off the surface with a shearing action. The chocolate will form curls. The thickness depends on the length of the shearing action and the angle of the knife. Make chocolate shavings in the same way, but let the chocolate set firmer.

CHOCOLATE TREE

Make a standing Christmas tree from cutouts by
cutting two shapes with a tree cutter. Cut one in half
with a hot sharp knife. Attach the whole tree to a
flat chocolate base using melted chocolate. Position
each half tree and attach with more melted chocolate.
Add silver dragées.

SIMPLE CUTTER SHAPES

Use biscuit (cookie) cutters to cut shapes from a
chocolate sheet. The simple shapes look good on
children's birthday cakes.

217

CHOCOLATE LEAVES

To make chocolate leaves, choose real leaves for moulds, such as those from roses or fuchsias which have well-defined veins. Pick the leaves, leaving a bit of stem to make handling easier. Wash and dry them well.

Melt the chocolate. Using a small paintbrush, thickly coat the underside of the leaf with melted chocolate. The coating should be smooth and fairly thick, and should come to the edge of the leaf but not overlap, or removing the leaf will be difficult. Place on waxed paper and leave in a cool place until set, which could take up to 1 hour.

When the chocolate is firm, carefully peel off the leaf and place the chocolate leaf on waxed or greaseproof paper. Store in a cool place until needed.

CHOCOLATE LEAF BIRTHDAY CAKE

Cover an oval cake with melted chocolate and leave to set. Arrange the chocolate leaves on the cake. Pipe the chocolate stems. Make the plaque from a mould and overpipe with white chocolate.

218

CHOCOLATE CONES

A chocolate cone can be used as a cake decoration or as an attractive party favour. The cones can be filled with marzipan fruit or figures, nuts, or small sweets.

Melt baker's chocolate in the usual way. Make a small paper piping bag and tape the seam. Stuff the bag with paper or some object to hold shape. Pour a thick coating of chocolate around the cone. When it is well covered, place it on a board with the flap side down. Leave in the container to hold the shape.

Use a thick paintbrush to stipple some more chocolate on the cone to give a log appearance. Leave in a cool room for several hours, or until the chocolate is firm.

When set, remove the container, and then remove the bag by peeling the edge away from the sides of the cone. Twist the bag between your fingers and gently pull it away from the chocolate.

MODELLING CHOCOLATE

This chocolate modelling compound can be used to make moulded flowers and figures. It is easy to work with and does not require any adhesives, as the moulded pieces will stick to each other. If there are any cracks, smooth over them with your finger. The modelling compound will keep for several weeks without refrigeration. Wrap it in plastic wrap and place in a plastic container stored in a cool place. When ready to work with the paste, cut off a piece and knead. Take care not to over-knead or the ingredients will separate. If it becomes too soft, put in a cool place until it becomes firm.

CHOCOLATE MODELLING COMPOUND

125 g (4 oz/4 squares) baker's chocolate
120 ml (4 fl oz/½ Cup) liquid glucose or corn syrup
Melt the chocolate in a double saucepan. Warm the liquid glucose or corn syrup and mix well with the chocolate. Wrap in plastic wrap, place in a plastic bag or container, and leave to set for at least one hour before modelling.

MOULDED ROSES

To use this modelling compound and achieve the best results, allow to rest in warm room for about an hour after making. When making the petals use only walnut-sized pieces at a time. Do not worry if it feels very greasy to the touch, this is because the warmth of the hand melts the cocoa butter in the chocolate. Mould a piece of the compound about the size of a little finger nail into a pear shape. Stand upright fat side down. Take a small piece of paste and roll between palms into a sausage shape. With thumb and forefinger of left hand, flatten out top piece of sausage. Hold the remainder with thumb and forefinger of right hand. Lay flattened edge in the palm of the hand with the tail pointing to outside edge of hand. With the thick end of a double ball tool, gently thin outside edge of petal. Hold petal with thumb and forefinger of left hand and with thumb and forefinger of right hand nip off surplus piece of sausage. The petals will be floppy, so lay flat on surface to set.

Make two petals about as big as thumb nail. Pick up centrepiece and lay on petal two-thirds to the left of it. Wrap left edge petal over centre. Take second petal and lay inside the first petal bringing round to overlap outside first petal. With thumb gently roll back outside edge of petals. The build-up of petals is as follows, tucking one inside the other until you have completed the sequence.

Bud – pear shape + 2 petals
Half rose – pear shape + 2 petals + 3 petals
Full rose – pear shape + 2 petals + 3 petals + 5 petals

Make each layer of petals slightly larger as they extend outwards.

PIPED SCROLLS AND SHELLS

To pipe chocolate scrolls or shells onto a cake, use a No7 or No43 star or shell tube in a medium bag. Fill a bag with piping chocolate and pipe the design onto the cake.

FILIGREE AND LACE

Piped chocolate lace or filigree pieces, also called off-pieces, can be used to decorate cakes or sweets. Place the design under waxed paper. Fill a bag with piping chocolate and cut off the tip to represent a No1 tube. Pipe the design. When set, slide a thin palette knife under each piece to release it.

Chocolate lace designs should have fewer joins than royal icing lace, as it is more difficult to stop and start when piping melted chocolate.

EMBROIDERY

Fill a small piping bag with melted chocolate and cut off the tip to represent a No0 or 1 tube. Pipe the design, working with one colour at a time. Leave to dry.

FREESTANDING CENTREPIECE

Melt some milk (sweet) chocolate; thicken with a little glycerine. Pipe four pieces of the design (page 252) onto greaseproof or waxed paper which has been well stuck down on the worksurface.

To assemble, lay a left-hand and right-hand piece on a piece of waxed paper and attach by piping melted chocolate down the centre. Fix the third side in the centre with melted chocolate, supporting gently. Count to ten to allow the chocolate to set.

With your fingertips, carefully lift the ornament upright. Fix the fourth side with melted chocolate and count to ten for it to set.

The filigree ornament can be placed on a cake, on a thin cake board or on a cut or moulded chocolate base. Attach in the centre with melted chocolate.

RUNOUTS

Choose pictures from children's books or colouring books, or draw your own. Place the design under waxed paper. Melt the chocolate and pour into a piping bag. Do not let the chocolate get too hot or it will overflow to the outside of the design. Cut off the tip. Make a very small hole for a small design; for a larger design, cut the tip to represent a No1 or 2 tube. Pipe the design carefully. For a figure, pipe the body from side to side. For an arm, start at the top and run the chocolate down towards the hand. When the runouts are set, slip a small palette knife underneath and carefully lift off the waxed paper. For fireman design, see page 252.

DECORATING IDEAS

COFFEE GÂTEAU

Coat a prepared cake in coffee-coloured and flavoured buttercream. The cake could be layered with coffee buttercream flavoured with a coffee-based liqueur such as Tia Maria. Comb-scrape the sides of the cake, and decorate the base with plain shells piped in chocolate buttercream. Rest a strip of waxed paper on the top of the chilled buttercream surface and pipe a straight line against it, remove the waxed paper. Using piping chocolate pipe the filigree in one half of the cake. Decorate the other half with small chocolate drops, made by piping melted chocolate onto waxed paper. A sugarpaste inscription plaque and some piped linework complete the gâteau.

PEACH AND CHOCOLATE GÂTEAU

Cover a sponge cake with peach buttercream. Use a comb-scraper to decorate the surface. Divide the top into 16 portions with a long knife or gâteau divider. Pipe a chocolate filigree heart for the centre decoration and 16 filigree pieces. Leave to set. Pipe a freehand S-scroll design on top and a shell round top and bottom edges with a No44 tube. Place heart and filigree pieces in position on the cake. Use a darker shade of peach to pipe the centre of the flowers with a No2 tube. Pipe additional decoration onto gâteau as shown.

GATEAU WITH CENTREPIECE

The filigree pieces can be made in advance but assemble them shortly before use, as this decoration is difficult to store.

Cover gâteau with natural coloured buttercream. The first layer of icing will contain crumbs so to make sure the second coat is smooth, put the cake in the refrigerator for 10 minutes. Remove and leave at room temperature for five minutes before re-coating. Use a comb scraper on the top and round the side. Pipe top and bottom shells with a No44 tube; overpipe with No3, then overpipe again.

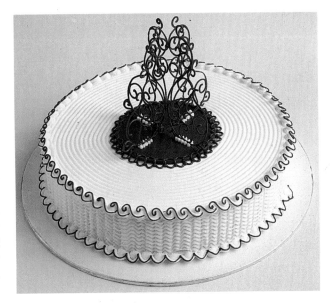

Melt some milk (sweet) chocolate; thicken with a little glycerine. Pipe four pieces of the design (page 252) onto greaseproof or waxed paper. For the disc, run out a sheet of chocolate on paper in a baking tin (pan). Cut out a round plaque. Leave to dry. Stick plaque to the gâteau as shown. Pipe a line and hold one piece in position with the central line straight. Place the opposite side in position, sticking the two together. Hold until set. Attach the other two pieces in position. Pipe bulbs of buttercream on the top for contrast.

CHOCOLATE BOXES

90 g (3 oz/⅓ Cup) butter
90 g (3 oz/⅓ Cup) caster (superfine) sugar
2 medium eggs, separated
90 g (3 oz/3 squares) plain (semisweet) chocolate, melted
30 g (1 oz/¼ Cup) cocoa powder
30 ml (6 teaspoons) hot water
30 g (1 oz/¼ Cup) ground almonds
60 g (2 oz/½ Cup) plain (all-purpose) flour, sifted

BUTTERCREAM
90 g (3 oz/⅓ Cup) unsalted (sweet) butter
250 g (8 oz/1 ½ Cups) icing (confectioner's) sugar, sifted·
6 teaspoons brandy

DECORATION
375 g (12 oz/12 squares) plain (semisweet) chocolate
24 silver or sugared almonds

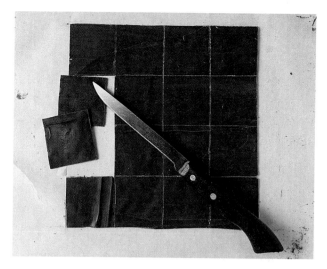

Grease and line a 20 cm (8 in) square cake tin (pan) with greaseproof (waxed) paper, grease paper. Heat the oven to 160C (325F/Gas 3). Put butter and sugar in a bowl and beat together until creamy. Add egg yolks then beat in melted chocolate. Mix cocoa with hot water until smooth then add to mixture. Fold in ground almonds and flour. Whisk egg whites until stiff then fold in. Turn the mixture into prepared tin (pan), level and bake for 25 minutes. Leave to cool a few minutes in the tin, then turn out and cool on a wire rack.

Meanwhile, make the buttercream by beating butter, icing (confectioner's) sugar and brandy together until creamy and smooth.

To make the decoration, melt chocolate and stir until smooth. Using two pieces of non-stick paper, spread chocolate in a thin even layer using a large palette knife, trying to keep to a rectangle to avoid wastage. Leave until just set but not hard. Cut 5 cm (2 in) squares using a sharp knife and ruler; 40 squares will be needed. When set, squares can be removed from paper.

To finish boxes, trim edges from cake. Cut in half and spread one piece with about one-third of the buttercream. Place other piece of cake on top, then cut into 8 squares. Put remaining buttercream into a piping bag fitted with a small star tube and pipe scrolls over the top of each cake.

Attach chocolate squares to sides of each cake using a small blob of remaining buttercream. Finally arrange 3 almonds on each cake and place a chocolate square on top at an angle to make a lid.

CHOCOLATE YULE LOG

3 large eggs
125 g (4 oz/½ Cup) caster (superfine) sugar
60 g (2 oz/½ Cup) plain (all-purpose) flour
30 g (1 oz/¼ Cup) cocoa powder
15 ml (3 teaspoons) hot water

BUTTERCREAM

155 g (5 oz/⅔ Cup) unsalted (sweet) butter
375 g (12 oz/2¼ Cups) icing (confectioner's) sugar, sifted
15 ml (3 teaspoons) milk
15 g (½ oz/2 tablespoons) cocoa
25–30 ml (5–6 teaspoons) boiling water

CHOCOLATE LEAVES

60 g (2 oz/2 squares) plain (semi-sweet) chocolate
30 g (1 oz/1 square) milk (sweet) chocolate
Holly or small rose leaves
Marzipan, optional

Grease and line a large Swiss (jelly) roll tin (pan) 33 x 23 cm (13 x 9 in) with greaseproof (waxed) paper. Heat the oven to 200C (400F/Gas 6).

Put eggs and sugar into a bowl and whisk until thick and mousse-like. Sift flour and cocoa powder twice, then carefully fold into egg mixture, then fold in water. Turn into prepared tin (pan) and bake for 8–10 minutes.

Place a sheet of greaseproof (waxed) paper on top of a damp tea-towel and sprinkle with caster sugar. Turn sponge upside down onto paper, peel off lining paper and trim edges. Quickly roll up with paper inside and leave to cool on a wire rack.

Meanwhile, make the buttercream by beating butter with icing (confectioner's) sugar and milk until smooth and creamy. Blend cocoa powder with hot water until smooth then cool.

Unroll cake and spread with one-third of buttercream. Re-roll and refrigerate for 30 minutes. Beat cocoa mixture into remaining buttercream.

Cut a short diagonal slice off one end of the roll and join it to side of cake using chocolate buttercream to resemble a branch. Place on a cake board and cover log with remaining chocolate buttercream and mark surface with a texture to look like bark of a tree. Sprinkle a little icing (confectioner's) sugar over to look like snow. Chill for 1 hour before serving.

To make chocolate leaves, melt both types of chocolate in separate bowls and stir until smooth. Using fresh undamaged leaves which have been washed and dried (it is advisable to soften holly leaves by soaking in hot water for 10 minutes), coat the underside using a fine paintbrush. Coat some with plain (semi-sweet) and others with milk (sweet) chocolate. Allow chocolate to dry, chocolate side up then give a second coat and allow to dry. When hard,

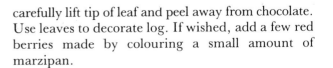

carefully lift tip of leaf and peel away from chocolate. Use leaves to decorate log. If wished, add a few red berries made by colouring a small amount of marzipan.

224

FESTIVE CHOCOLATE CARROT CAKE

150 ml (6 fl oz/¾ Cup) sunflower oil
150 g (6 oz/¾ Cup) soft light brown sugar
3 medium eggs
15 ml (1 teaspoon) vanilla essence (extract)
125 g (4 oz/1 Cup) walnuts, chopped
250 g (8 oz/2 Cups) carrots, grated
150 g (6 oz/1½ Cups) plain (all-purpose) flour
30 g (1 oz/¼ Cup) cocoa powder
5 ml (1 teaspoon) baking powder
5 ml (1 teaspoon) bicarbonate of soda
Pinch salt

ICING (FROSTING)
250 g (8 oz/8 squares) plain (semi-sweet) chocolate
155 g (5 oz/⅔ Cup) unsalted (sweet) butter
125 g (4 oz/¾ Cup) icing (confectioner's) sugar

DECORATION
30 g (1 oz/1 square) plain (semi-sweet) chocolate
60 g (2 oz/2 squares) white chocolate

Grease and line a deep 20 cm (8 in) round cake tin (pan) with greaseproof (waxed) paper and lightly grease. Heat oven to 180C (350F/Gas 4).

Put oil, sugar, eggs and vanilla essence into a large bowl and beat until well blended. Add nuts, carrots and stir together. Sieve dry ingredients then fold into mixture. Turn into the prepared tin and level surface. Bake for about 1 hour, test with a skewer. Turn out of tin and cool on a wire rack.

Make the icing by melting chocolate, while still warm, beat in butter and icing (confectioner's) sugar. Cool and beat occasionally, until easy to spread. Meanwhile, melt plain (semi-sweet) chocolate for the decoration and spread thickly on a piece of non-stick paper. Leave until set, but not too hard, then using a small star-shaped cutter, cut out shapes, dip cutter in hot water and dry quickly to ensure that the tips of the stars do not break. When set, they can be lifted off the paper.

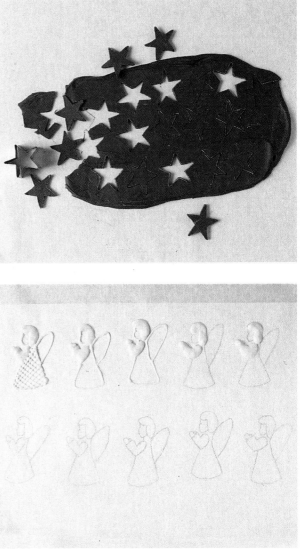

To make angels, draw or trace outline of angel (page 251), about 7.5 cm (3 in) high onto plain paper, cover with a piece of non-stick paper. Melt white chocolate and put into a paper piping bag fitted with a No1 tube. Pipe outline of angels then either completely fill in or pipe a lattice effect within outline. Pipe about 12–16 angels. Allow to set then remove from paper.

To finish cake, spread half of icing over top and around the sides of cake. Put remainder into piping bag fitted with a star tube and pipe rosettes around top of the cake and place chocolate star in each. Attach angels around sides of cake, refrigerate for 1 hour to set.

MODELLING

Children and the young at heart love novelty cakes. Children's cakes decorated with animals or cartoon characters are always a great hit while it can be fun to pick out a hobby or even poke fun at someone's foibles through a model on a cake. The skills are basically the same whether sugarpaste or marzipan is used although the appearance is different with sugarpaste looking finer than marzipan.

The three cakes here have been devised with teenagers in mind – always a difficult age group to please. The hamburger cake is made from two small fruit cakes and then decorated and accompanied by modelled french fries in a box. The car is modelled over the basic cake shape and the bin cake is modelled over the cake and the figure made from sugarpaste.

MODELLING

Marzipan and sugarpaste can be used to model all sorts of shapes and figures to decorate cakes. Figure modelling is easy once the basic shapes have been learned, and even children can quickly create interesting and attractive models.

Use white marzipan for modelling, as it takes colour well. Homemade marzipan can be used, but commercial paste tends to be less sticky. Sugarpaste is easy to model and will roll without cracking, but because it is very soft, only simple, small figures can be made. If making more complicated figures, add gum tragacanth to make the paste stronger and more pliable. Use 5 ml (1 teaspoon) for 250 g (8 oz) sugarpaste, knead thoroughly, then place in a plastic bag and rest for 2 hours before using.

When assembling figures, stick pieces together with a little egg white or with melted chocolate. Do not use cocktail sticks (toothpicks) or wires on figures for children's cakes or party favours.

EQUIPMENT

Only a minimal amount of equipment is necessary for modelling, and often household tools can be adapted if special tools are unavailable. Most useful are a nonstick worksurface and rolling pin; sharp kitchen knife; and a ball modelling tool. A crochet hook can be used instead of a ball tool. Other modelling tools are available from cake decorating shops or from craft shops. Many tools used by potters are useful for marzipan modelling, as the techniques are quite similar. All of the marzipan and sugarpaste figures are made using the same basic shapes. Practise each shape before trying out the figures. It is useful to measure out each piece so that you learn to recognize a 15 g (½ oz) ball, cone, etc, as this will help you to keep the pieces for each figure in proportion.

HAND POSITIONS FOR MODELLING

1   *This is the position on the hand where most of the figures are modelled.*

2   *To form a point on a ball to make a cone shape, place the ball at the base of your palm. The cone shape is formed at the base of the palms by moving your hands backwards and forwards.*

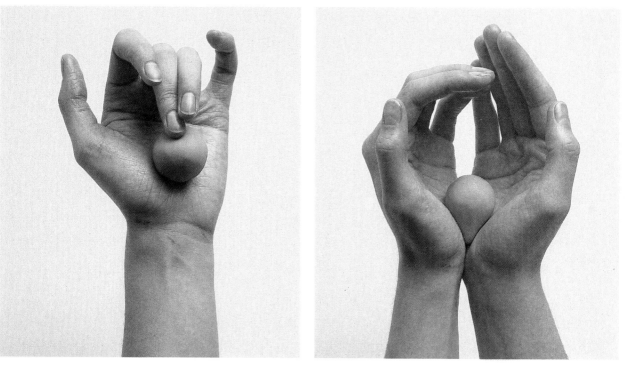

3 *To make an elongated cone, as for the elephant's trunk, have your hands as far apart as possible with your elbows tightly tucked by your hips. With the bases of your palms together, move your hands backwards and forwards.*

4 *To make a sausage, first make a ball. Place the ball on the worksurface and roll to a sausage shape using two fingers, then three fingers.*

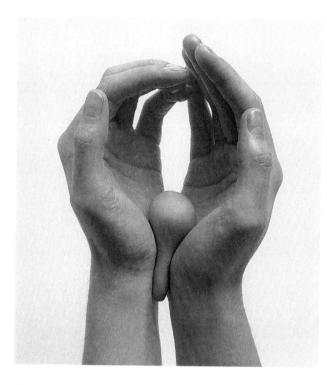

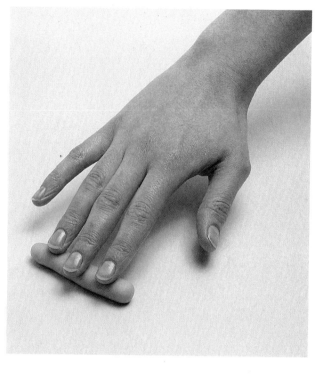

5 *To make the butterbean shape, place a ball in the palm of your hands and use a finger to gently roll into a butterbean.*

6 *To make indentations for the eye sockets, hold the head in one hand and the ball tool in the other hand. Press the ball tool in firmly. Move the handle of the ball tool upwards and remove.*

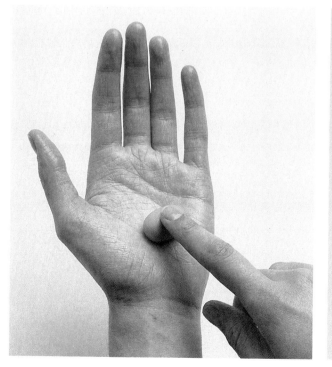

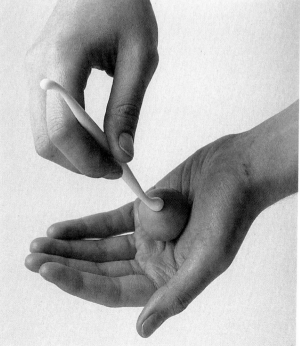

MARZIPAN FRUIT

Realistic models of every fruit and vegetable in the garden can be made from marzipan. Miniature models can be used to decorate cakes or boxes for attractive gifts, while larger models, up to life-sized, make lovely table decorations.

When modelling fruit and vegetables, try to work with the natural one in front of you to get the correct shape and colour. Marzipan models can be any size, so long as all the fruit or vegetables to be used in an arrangement are of the same proportions. Other fruit and vegetables may be made using those given here as a guide.

GRAPES

Colour the marzipan either raspberry or pale green. For each grape, make a ball, then use a finger to roll it into shape between a ball and a cone. Make several and arrange on a marzipan triangle base. Build up the grapes in layers to make a realistic bunch. Make a pale brown stalk, lift out a grape at the end, position the stalk and press in the grape.

APPLE

Make a pale green ball, and make indentations in the top and bottom with the end of a paintbrush. Use the back of a knife to make a small cross in the top and bottom. Cut a clove in two and use one piece for the stem and the other for the calyx. Paint in the red markings.

PEAR

Colour the marzipan either pale green or yellow. Make a ball, then make it into a pear shape by rolling gently between the heels of your hands. Make an indentation in the top. For the stalk, make a small, tapered brown sausage.

SATSUMA OR CLEMENTINE

Make an orange ball with an indentation at the top for the stem. Press the ball with a nutmeg grater to get the mottled effect. Use a clove for the stalk, or make three tiny, brown, tapered sausages and press in with a cocktail stick (toothpick).

ORANGE

Make a larger ball, either round or slightly oval. Mark with a grater, indent with a ball tool and mark a star shape with the back of a knife.

The fruits in this crystal bowl are three-quarter models of life-sized ones. To assemble the arrangement, be sure that all the fruit is thoroughly dry, then pile into an attractive display. Use melted chocolate to hold them together, if necessary.

LEMON

Make a fat yellow sausage, then use a finger and thumb to stroke up one end gently. Mark the skin with a grater. Colour the other end with green food colouring or petal dust, then add a stalk.

GRAPEFRUIT

Make a yellow ball, then flatten the top. Indent with a ball tool. Use the back of a knife to mark a star, then place a pale brown marzipan ball in the indentation. Mark the skin with a grater.

PEACH

Make a ball of pale peach-coloured marzipan. Use the back of a knife to mark a line down one side. Use cotton wool (cotton) to apply pale pink colour on either side of the line. When the colour is dry, brush on the bloom with cotton wool dipped in cornflour (cornstarch).

BANANA

Colour the marzipan yellow with a touch of brown and make a sausage with slightly tapered ends. Bend towards you, then shape the sides with the back of a knife. Colour the ends with dark brown food colouring and touch with a little green. Paint in the streaks and a few brown marks.

MARZIPAN FIGURES

Figure modelling is one of the most delightful of all the sugarcraft skills. All of the charming animals and human figures here and on the following pages are made using the basic shape and hand positions. Each marzipan model should be an individual character. Use the different facial expressions and hats to create the humorous personalities and interesting characters.

CAT

1 *For the body, make a cone with 15 g (½ oz) white marzipan. Attach a long, tapered sausage for the tail.*

2 *Make a 5 g (⅙ oz) ball for the head. Gently pinch up the ears and indent with a ball tool. Make indentations for the eyes and pipe. Mark whiskers with a knife. Add small nose and mouth of pink marzipan.*

3 *For a different face, use thumb and forefinger to gently stroke out sides of face, then snip with sharp scissors for whiskers. Finish as for other face and attach head to body.*

Once the basic figure is mastered, adapt the poses and features to create a range of individual characters.

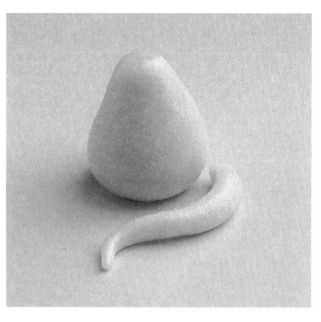

MOUSE

1 Make a 5 g (⅙ oz) cone for the head and indent for eyes. The nose is a tiny pink ball. For the ears, make two tiny balls, position on the head, and indent with a ball tool. Alternatively, indent before placing on head, position pink balls for the inside, then position and indent again. Pipe eyes.

2 Make a 15 g (½ oz) cone for the body. The feet are small flattened cones. Snip for the toes, then place under body.

3 Make a tiny sausage for each arm. Taper the top end, then flatten the other end for the hand. Snip for fingers and place around body.

CHICK

1 For the body, make a ball with 15 g (½ oz) yellow marzipan. Indent the centre for the head to sit.

2 Head is a 4 g (⅐ oz) ball. Make indentation for the eyes.

3 Roll out red marzipan into a flat strip. Cut a diagonal from the end, then cut diagonally for a diamond-shaped beak. Press a cocktail stick (toothpick) into the centre of the diamond and press in for the mouth. Cut triangles from strip and attach to top of head for comb. Pipe eyes.

DUCK

1 For the body, take 10 g (⅓ oz) white marzipan and roll into a cone in the base of the hands. Mark tail feathers with a knife and turn up. Make an indentation for the head to rest in.

2 Head is a 4 g (⅐ oz) ball. Make indentations for the eyes with a ball tool. Make a tiny orange carrot for the beak and attach to the head with the fat side up.

3 Make a small orange sausage for the feet and bend into a V-shape. Flatten the ends and mark for the webbed feet. Attach under body. Pipe eyes.

KOALA

1   *The body is made from two cones. Make a 25 g (¾ oz) brown cone, and use your finger to make an indentation in the centre. Press in a 5 g (⅙ oz) white cone and roll them together. Flatten the top to take the head.*

2   *Make a 10 g (⅓ oz) sausage for the legs. Indent for feet, cut lengthwise, press up feet, mark paws and attach. Make a 5 g (⅙ oz) sausage for the arms, indent for paws, cut lengthwise, mark claws and position.*

3   *Make a 10 g (⅓ oz) ball for the head. Squeeze and stroke the sides, then snip with scissors for the fur. Make two small brown balls for the ears. Flatten, then indent them and place smaller white balls in the indentation. Attach, then indent again. Squeeze the outside edges, then snip with scissors. Eyes are tiny black marzipan balls; nose is a black oval.*

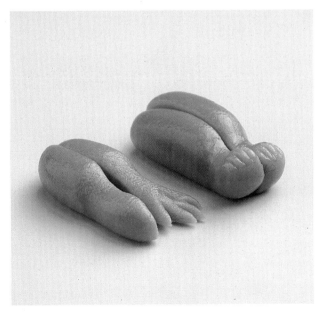

TEDDY BEAR

1   *Colour the marzipan yellow with a touch of brown. For the body, make a cone with 20 g (⅔ oz) and flatten the top slightly for the head.*

2   *For the legs, make a sausage with 5 g (⅙ oz). Indent with the little finger. Cut in half lengthwise, turn up the feet and attach legs to body. Mark claws with the back of a knife. Make arms as for legs, but smaller.*

3   *For the head, make a cone with 10 g (⅓ oz) marzipan. Cut mouth with a sharp knife, place the knife point inside and press down to open. Squeeze sides of the mouth to make a smile. Make indentations with a ball tool for the eye sockets. For the ears, make tiny balls and attach. Place a finger behind each ear and indent with a ball tool. Make a tiny brown oval and position on the end of the nose. Pipe eyes.*

PANDA

Make a 25 g (¾ oz) cone of white marzipan for the body and flatten the top to take the head.

Make a 10g (⅓ oz) black sausage for the legs. Indent twice for the muscle and the paws. Cut lengthwise, turn up the paws and attach legs to the body. Make a black sausage with 5 g (⅙ oz) for the arms and make as for the legs.

The head is a 10 g (⅓ oz) white cone. The eyes are tiny black rectangles cut from rolled marzipan. Attach a black oval nose. The ears are small black balls. Indent with a ball tool after attaching

ELEPHANT

Make a fat sausage with 50 g (1½ oz) of pink marzipan for the body and legs. Cut at both ends and separate for the legs. Bend to shape. Make indentations with ball tool for the toes. Attach a small, flattened cone for the tail.

For the head, make a 30 g (1 oz) cone and elongate for the trunk. Bend the trunk up. Cut the mouth with a knife, and indent the eye sockets with a ball tool,

For the ears, make two balls. Make indentations with your finger, leaving a ridge around the top edge, and attach the ears to the sides of the head. Pipe the eyes.

HUMAN FIGURES

Moulds are available for making modelled figures but more individual and lifelike results are gained by making them freehand which ensures that no two figures are alike. Each one takes on the personality of its own as choices of pose, features, dress and size are made.

Because the figures do vary in size and shape, the clothes patterns need to be adapted individually. Make the paste garments larger than needed so that the paste can be trimmed to shape as it is being draped around the form.

As the figure is dressed, it will increase in size, therefore the paste should be kept as thin as possible. Also the body shape should start off narrow to allow for the bulk of added clothes.

Accurate figure proportions are important. The head should measure one-sixth of the body height. In the case of a child, however, the head size is a little larger. Arms with outstretched fingers reach to mid-thigh.

Painting the features: Eyes should focus on an object within the scene so they don't seem vacant or staring. Indent the socket and whiten. When dry paint the coloured iris. Dry, then place the pupil inside. A white dot can be added for a highlight. Carefully outline with a very fine brush, then add lashes and brows.

Blush the cheeks with dusting powder. Paint lips a pale paprika colour; not bright pink or red.

Pipe hair with royal icing; or make by pushing soft paste through a garlic press or sieve. Alternatively, roll very thin sausages of paste into fine strands. This last method looks effective but is time-consuming.

Each modelled part must be allowed to dry completely, otherwise it will crack and disintegrate when you try to dress it.

CHOIR BOY

Shape a white cone for the surplice. Make a red sausage for the underskirt and flatten to the correct size. Attach underskirt to cone with egg white or gum arabic glue

Make a long white sausage for arms. Measure against figure to obtain the correct length. Thin down the sausage where it crosses neck. Make indentations at the end of each arm. Make hands by rolling two small, flesh-coloured sausages. Flatten and curve with ball tool; place into indentations. Roll a flesh-coloured ball for the head.

Make a frilled collar with a small carnation cutter. Frill edge with a cocktail stick (toothpick). Place on body. Attach head. Make hair by cutting out a piece of yellow paste with a medium blossom cutter. Paint in eyes, nose and mouth. Roll out a thin white rectangle for the song sheet.

FAIRY OR ANGEL

1 *Head is a small ball of flesh-coloured paste. Hair and features are as for choir boy.*

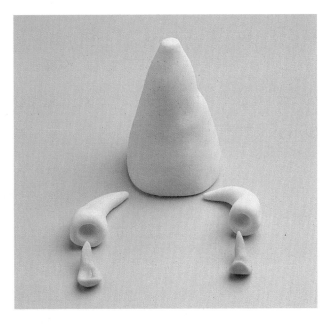

2 *Make a white cone for body. For arms, make two sausages from white paste, taper one end for shoulder. Indent sleeve end for hands. Model hands; completely curl one hand to hold the wand, which is made of florist's wire with a tiny cutout sugarpaste star stuck on the end.*

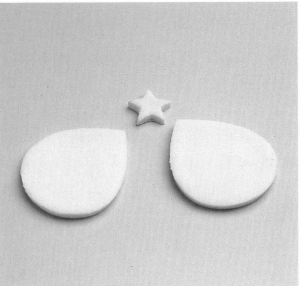

3 *Cut wings from white paste using a large rose petal cutter. Attach to back of cone with royal icing. Decorate edges of dress with piped dots of royal icing.*

239

MOULDS

There are a wide selection of commercially available moulds that make modelling a very simple process. Use sugarpaste kneaded with gum tragacanth and press very firmly into the mould then trim off any excess paste. Ease a cocktail stick (toothpick) into the back of the mould to release the sugarpaste and allow to dry for 4 to 24 hours, depending on the size and thickness of the mould. Paint and attach to the cake when dry.

Homemade moulds may be easily made from one of the many compounds found in craft stores. These give greater freedom and flexibility and provide an ideal way of producing a special image for a cake decoration.

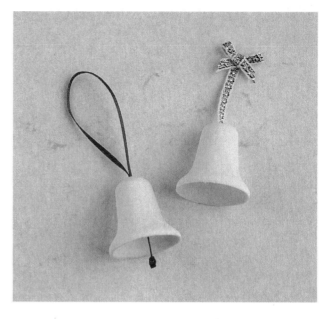

BELLS

Bells, plain or filled with flowers, can replace a tall vase of flowers on a wedding cake. Many different bell moulds are commercially available, or make your own from Christmas decorations and even budgie bells.

1   *Dust the inside of the mould with cornflour (cornstarch). Roll out paste to about 10 mm (⅓ in) thick.*

2   *Press paste into mould. Push into the centre of the mould. Continue pushing until paste has taken the shape of the inside of the bell. Keep taking paste in and out to be sure it is not sticking. If necessary dust the inside of the mould again with cornflour (cornstarch).*

3   *Use a small sharp knife to trim away excess paste. Use your index finger to smooth the edge of the paste to a fine edge. Leave bell in the mould for about 10 minutes before turning out to dry. Leave 6 hours before decorating.*

FATHER CHRISTMAS FACE

1 *Colour paste a flesh colour. Roll into a ball larger than the cavity of the mould. Dust inside of mould with cornflour (cornstarch). Press ball of paste into prepared mould. Trim off excess paste if necessary.*

2 *Use a cocktail stick (toothpick) pushed into back of paste to release from the mould. The turned-out face must be left to dry for at least 4 hours.*

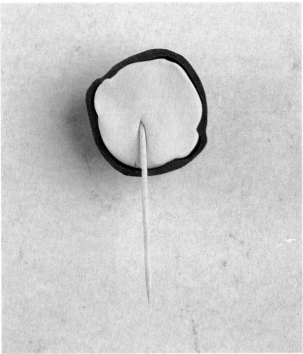

3 *Pink petal dust gives a warm glow to cheeks and nose. Use white petal dust with a little clear spirit to paint eyes. Finish with blue, then black pupils. Lips are painted red, then outlined with pale brown. Hat is a triangle of red sugarpaste moulded to head.*

4 *Finish face by piping beard, moustache, eyebrows, fur and pompom with white royal icing. Use a No1 tube and work on one area at a time. Use a small dry paintbrush to texture icing. Stick onto a plaque or directly onto the cake with royal icing.*

PASTILLAGE CARDS

It is important to dry the pieces on a completely flat surface, lightly dusted with cornflour (cornstarch). Roll some paste out thinly. Cut the card shape on the surface on which it is to be dried. Do not attempt to lift and transfer the piece after any cutout shapes have been removed, as this could distort the overall shape. Cut the card shape with a very sharp knife. Use a single rocking movement, do not drag the knife as this will stretch and distort the paste. Cut in from the corners, not out to the corners. Dry the pieces flat so that they do not warp.

HEART-SHAPED CARD

Cut out card pieces as above. Use a biscuit cutter to remove the heart shape from the front card. Cut a heart shape in paste, medium thickness, place on inside face. Smooth the edge with fingers and modelling tool to give a padded effect. Paint a monogram on the inside of the raised heart. Pipe an edge with royal icing around the padded heart on the inside and also round the cutout heart edge.

TO ASSEMBLE CARDS

Pipe a snailstrail using a No0 or No1 piping tube along the inside edge of the card. Place the two pieces of the card together. Support until dry. Pipe another decorative edging on the spine of the card to strengthen.

242

DECORATING IDEAS

HUMPTY DUMPTY CAKE

Take a chocolate sponge cake made in a loaf tin (pan) and coat with chocolate buttercream. Melt some chocolate and spread out on a sheet of waxed paper using a palette knife. Allow to set and cut into brick shapes. Attach to cake. Make the Humpty Dumpty from 155 g (5 oz) marzipan. Make an egg shape for the body, two sausage shapes for the legs and two smaller sausages for the arms. Make the clothing, ladybird, snail and flowers using the photograph as a guide. The pieces should stick together naturally, but if they do not, then attach with small dabs of chocolate.

ANIMAL FUN CAKE

Make a numeral cake in a novelty tin (pan) or cut from a square sponge cake with cream-coloured sugarpaste and leave for 24 hours. Meanwhile make a selection of animals for the top of the cake. Use the animals given at the beginning of the chapter or make other animals from pictures using the same principles. Leave to dry and harden. Decorate the sides of the cake using chocolate matchsticks and attaching to the cake with dabs of melted chocolate to represent the fence. Carefully arrange the animals on top of the cake securing with melted chocolate.

GOLDEN WEDDING CAKE

Cover a heart-shaped cake with ivory sugarpaste and leave to skin. Make the cherub using a mould and paint with gold lustre colour mixed to a paint consistency with clear spirit such as gin or vodka. The top is finished with a small plunger blossom cutter and an inscription. The side frills are cut with a plain pastry cutter and attached with egg white. The dots made with a No0 tube are piped around the frills. The cake is finished with a ribbon.

BIG SNAX BURGER CAKE

20 cm (8 in) round light fruit cake, marzipanned. (Before baking, remove 2 heaped tablespoons mixture for burger buns. Divide between two 10 cm (4 in) Yorkshire pudding tins (muffin pans). Cook with main cake for about 20 minutes.)
1 kg (2½ lbs) sugarpaste
1 egg white, beaten
250 g (8 oz) modelling paste
450 g (8 oz/1¾ Cups) royal icing
Apricot jam (jelly)
375 g (12 oz) marzipan
Sesame seeds
Red, yellow, brown, black, green food colouring

Cover the cake with 750 g (1½ lb) white sugarpaste. Colour 185 g (6 oz) of sugarpaste red. Roll out to 20 cm (8 in) square and cut edge with a fancy cutter or a pastry wheel. Brush a little egg white on cake and place red sugarpaste cloth on top. Roll out modelling paste and use half to line a 13 cm (5 in) saucer. Cut the other into oblongs 6.5 x 6 cm (2¾ x 2½); two oblongs 6.5 x 3 cm (2¾ x 1¼ in); and one oblong 5.75 x 3 cm (2¼ x 1¼ in). Leave overnight to harden. The next day paint the edge of the sugarpaste plate with blue colouring. Paint the box sides with yellow stripes. When dry, join the box together with royal icing.

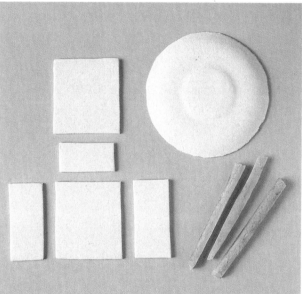

To make the burger bun, take the two small cakes and put one aside for the lid. Trim the other to make a flat base. Colour 125 g (4 oz) sugarpaste with yellow and brown to the colour of bread rolls. Roll out. Brush cakes with apricot jam (jelly) and cover with sugarpaste. Brush top of bun with a little brown colouring mixed with water to give a browned effect. Sprinkle with sesame seeds.

To make the burger, take 125 g (4 oz) marzipan and colour with brown and black food colouring. Shape into a round and pinch surface to give an uneven texture. Allow to dry a little and then pinch again to make surface cracks. Take 125 g (4 oz) marzipan and colour with yellow and a little brown to give a golden chip colour. Roll out thickly and cut into 'French fries'. Leave to dry. Take 30 g (1 oz) marzipan and colour green. Mould with the hands to make ragged edged pieces of lettuce. Colour the remaining marzipan yellow and roll out to 10 cm (4 in) square.

Take a little of the royal icing, colour it red and thin it to the consistency of double (heavy) cream. Using white royal icing to attach the pieces, assemble the cake as follows. Put the plate on the red cloth slightly off centre. Put burger bun on plate. Top with hamburger, lettuce and cheese. Drizzle over the red icing. Place burger bun on top. Fix French fry box at side of plate and fill with fries. Divide remaining royal icing in half and colour one half red. Use to pipe alternate blobs around base of cake.

CAR CAKE

20 cm (8 in) square rich or light fruit cake, marzipanned
2-egg quantity basic sponge cake baked in 550 g (2 lb) loaf
  tin (pan)
1.5 kg (3 lbs) sugarpaste
Green, yellow, red, black, blue and silver food colouring
125 g (4 oz) marzipan
Apricot jam (jelly)
250 g (8 oz/1 ¾ Cups) royal icing

Place the cake on a board. Colour 1 kg (2 lb) of sugarpaste pale green. Roll out and use to cover the cake. Colour 125 g (4 oz) sugarpaste grey, roll out in a wide strip and use to make a road. Moisten with a little water and place diagonally on the cake. Roll out 125 g (4 oz) sugarpaste and cut out small circles, triangles, and oblongs for road signs. Paint the shapes using food colours and a paintbrush. When dry, attach to sides of cake with royal icing.

To make the car, cut the sponge in a car shape as shown. Make two grooves under the car where the wheels will go. Shape two oblong blocks of marzipan twice the depth of the grooves, spread a little jam (jelly) in the grooves and put in the blocks; the car should now stand slightly off the ground.

Colour 185 g (6 oz) sugarpaste yellow. Brush cake with jam (jelly) and cover with yellow icing. Colour some sugarpaste black. Roll out thickly and using a small round cutter stamp out four wheels. Dry.

Colour some sugarpaste pale grey or blue and cut out six windows. Attach to cake using egg white. For headlights roll out two small sugarpaste balls and flatten slightly. Colour some sugarpaste grey and cut out two sets of bumpers (fenders) and grilles for the back of the car. Attach the wheels to the car. Shape the wings out of yellow sugarpaste and attach to the car over the wheels. Attach the headlights, bumpers, and grilles. Paint centres of wheels, bumpers, headlights, and grilles with silver food colour. Colour some royal icing yellow and using a small writing tube, outline the windows, doors and bonnet (hood) of car. With black icing pipe on windscreen (windshield) wipers.

Position car on cake. Colour remaining royal icing green and pipe round top edge and base of cake.

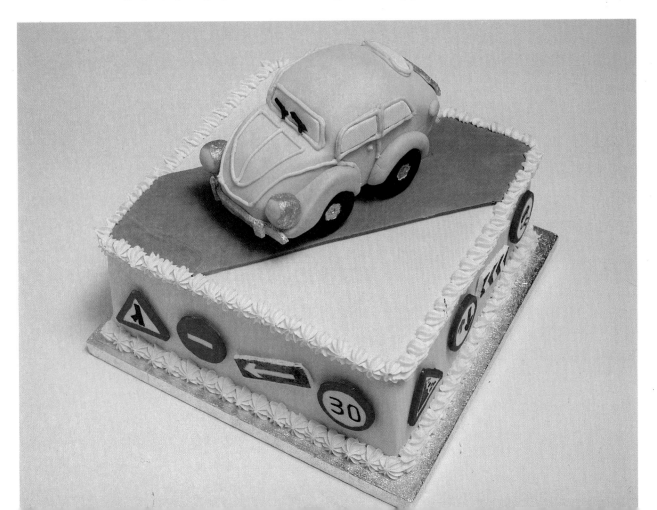

GARBAGE PATCH KID CAKE

Two 13 cm (5 in) deep round sponge cakes, each made using
2-egg quantity basic sponge mix
Apricot jam (jelly)
1 kg (2 lbs) sugarpaste
Blue, black, brown, red and yellow food colouring
250 g (8 oz) marzipan
Icing (confectioner's) sugar
250 g (8 oz/1 ¾ Cups) royal icing
Sweets (candies)

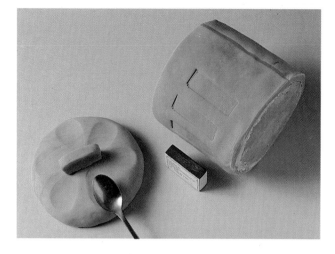

Cut the rounded tops off both cakes and reserve one for the lid. Sandwich the two cakes together with jam (jelly). Colour the sugarpaste with blue and black, do not over-knead, but leave it looking a little streaky. Brush the cake and lid with jam. Roll out sugarpaste and use to cover dustbin (garbage can) and lid. Using the non-striking side of a matchbox dusted with icing (confectioner's) sugar, make indentations around the side of the dustbin. Using the back of a teaspoon, make indentations in lid. Make a small handle and attach to dustbin lid.

Colour pieces of marzipan and model body parts as shown. Put the cake on a board. Position the body leaning against side of cake. Squeeze marzipan through a garlic press to represent hair (see page 169) and drape over head. Place half-eaten sweet (candy) in hands of body. Lean dustbin lid against cake, securing with royal icing. Fill dustbin with sweets attached with royal icing. Scatter a few empty wrappers around the base of cake.

TEMPLATES

Butterfly Beauty Cake (page 29)

Filigree Cradle (page 206)

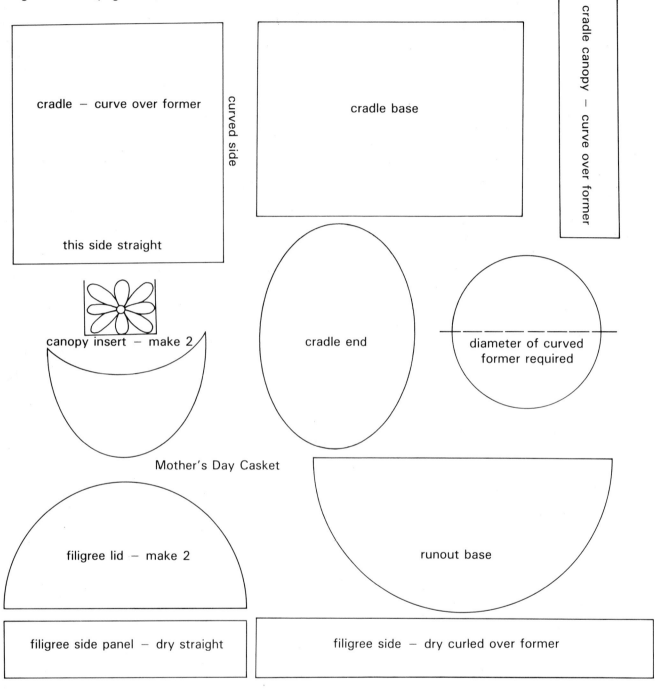

cradle — curve over former

curved side

this side straight

cradle base

cradle canopy — curve over former

canopy insert — make 2

cradle end

diameter of curved former required

Mother's Day Casket

filigree lid — make 2

runout base

filigree side panel — dry straight

filigree side — dry curled over former

White Wedding Cake (page 144)

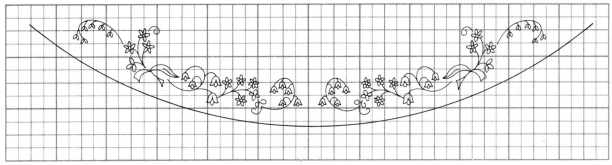

Filigree and Lace Pieces (pages 200-204)

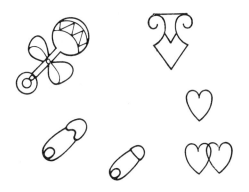
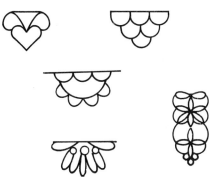

249

Lace Cake (page 210)

Butterfly Petal Cake (page 211)

Lace design

Trellis Work Heart (page 204)

ghosts

moon

All Hallows Cake (page 169)

First Birthday Cake (page 107)

Festive Chocolate Carrot
Cake (page 223)

1

witch

Chocolate Runout Fireman (page 221)

Freestanding Centrepiece (pages 221 and 222)

Happy Birthday Cake (page 140)

40 Cake (page 139)

Happy
Birthday

Good
Luck

Welcome
Baby

Happy
Birthday

Merry
Christmas

Easter
Greetings

New Year
Greetings

Congratulations

12345
67890

A B C D E F G H I J K L
M N O P Q R
S T U V W X Y Z

Lettering (pages 132–138)

INDEX

ACKNOWLEDGEMENTS

Photography on pages 114, 115, 134 by Lindsay John Bradshaw; 8, 11, 12, 13, 14, 15, 16, 17, 20, 21, 23, 24, 25, 26, 32, 33, 34, 35, 44, 45, 46, 47, 48, 49, 54, 55, 56, 57, 59, 60, 66, 68, 69, 70, 71, 72, 73, 79, 81, 82, 83, 84, 85, 86, 87, 93, 94, 95, 96, 97, 98, 99, 101, 103, 104, 105, 110, 111, 112, 113, 116, 117, 118, 119, 120, 121, 122, 123, 124, 125, 126, 127, 132, 133, 135, 136, 137 (top right), 144, 145, 146, 147, 148, 149, 150, 151, 152, 153, 158, 159, 177, 178, 179, 180, 181, 184, 185, 186, 187, 188, 189, 190, 193, 194, 195, 198, 199, 200, 201, 202, 203, 204, 205, 206, 207, 208, 209, 214, 215, 216, 217, 218, 219, 220, 221, 228, 229, 230, 232, 233, 234, 235, 236, 237, 239, 240, 241, 242, 243 by Melvin Gray and Graham Tann; 137 (top left and bottom left and right), 138 by John Todd of Carlton Studios and John Johnson

Food preparation on pages 48 (top), 49, 215, 216, 217, 218, 220 (top and bottom), 221 (bottom), 228, 229, 230, 232, 233, 234, 235, 236, 237 by Pat Ashby; 27, 28, 29, 61, 62, 63, 244, 245, 246 by Val Barrett; 4 cakes on jacket by Alison Birch; 114, 115, 134, 137 (top left, bottom left and right), 138 by Lindsay John Bradshaw; 36, 37, 38, 39 by Deborah Gray; 93, 94, 95, 96, 98 (middle left and right and bottom), 99 (top and middle), 123, 124, 125, 127 (bottom) by Norma Laver; 8, 11, 12, 13, 14, 15, 16, 17, 20, 21, 23, 24, 25, 26, 32, 33, 34, 35, 44, 45, 46, 47, 48 (bottom), 54, 55, 56, 57, 59, 66, 68, 69, 70 (top), 71, 79, 81, 82, 83 (top and bottom left), 84, 86, 97, 98 (top left and right), 104 (left), 110, 113, 116, 117, 118, 119, 121, 122, 126, 133, 135, 136, 145, 147, 148, 150, 151, 153 (bottom), 162, 163, 173, 174, 175, 176, 177, 178, 179, 180, 181, 182, 183, 184, 185, 186, 187, 188, 189, 190, 193, 194, 195, 198, 199, 200, 201, 202, 203, 204, 205, 206, 207, 208, 209, 214, 219, 220 (middle), 221 (top), 222, 240, 241, 242 (top), 243 by Nicholas Lodge; 73 (top), 87, 137, (top right), 144, 158, 161, 165 (bottom), 166, 242 (bottom right) by Elaine MacGregor; 60, 73 (bottom), 83 (bottom right), 85, 99 (bottom), 101, 103, 104 (right), 105, 111, 112, 120, 127 (top), 132, 242 (top) by Dolly Meers, Brenda Purton, Jenny Ridgwell, Ann Tann and Jenny Walker; 74, 75, 128, 129, 154, 155, 191, 192 by Janice Murfitt; 50 by Ann Nichol; 223, 224, 225 by Lorna Rhodes; 106, 139, 140, 141, 210, 211 by Bernadette Riddoch; 70 (bottom), 72, 146, 149, 152, 153 (top left and right), 159, 160, 164, 165 (top), 238, 239 by Anne Smith; 107 by Cynthia Venn